RECOVERY

Starr Daily

Author of

Love Can Open Prison Doors
Release
Wellsprings of Immortality

Martino Publishing
Mansfield Centre, CT
2014

Martino Publishing
P.O. Box 373,
Mansfield Centre, CT 06250 USA

ISBN 978-1-61427-618-0

Cover design by T. Matarazzo

Printed in the United States of America On 100% Acid-Free Paper

RECOVERY

Starr Daily

Author of

Love Can Open Prison Doors

Release

Wellsprings of Immortality

MACALESTER PARK PUBLISHING COMPANY
Saint Paul, Minnesota

RECOVERY

First Edition, 1948

Printed in the United States of America by
Macalester Park Publishing Company,
1571 Grand Avenue, Saint Paul 5, Minnesota

Dedication . . . . . .

To the shut-ins and sufferers of the world, this book is dedicated. May all who read take Hope, find Faith, and know Love.

TABLE OF CONTENTS

RECOVERY

THE REVEREND ROLAND J. BROWN

Introduction . . . .

"THE BOOK & THE MAN"

If you are afraid of losing your doubts don't read very far into this book. It is deadly to unbelief. If you have been in a secular college or a theological seminary long enough to have read and reasoned your primitive faith away, you had better shy clear of this document of modern miracles, for it will either convert you or condemn you. If you are a current Twentieth Century cynic and skeptic, and you are proud of your supercivilized pagan culture, beware of this thin volume, for if you so much as touch its jacket you are flirting with death—death to your old attitudes and marginal systems of thought.

This is a book of miracles, a document of answered prayers. It tells the story of a minister who takes Jesus literally, at his word, and how it changes him from a mediocre moralist and sermonizer into a miracle worker, like the Apostles of old.

A casual examination of the Four Gospels reveals the ministry as a trinitarian program of preaching, teaching, and healing. This ministry was exemplified by Jesus, and before and after Pentecost it was carried on by his disciples. Their calling to the ministry embraced this threefold commission. Whether the same commission was modified by the later disciples I am not prepared to say. I do know that we still have Christian ministers. Apparently they are *called* to the ministry, and are commissioned even as were the original group. They have developed the preaching and teaching ministry to a high degree. But that part most emphasized by Jesus, namely, the healing ministry, has well-nigh vanished from the regular Christian Church. Healing is no longer done to the glory of God as a witness to man. Only here and there is a minister found with Love and Faith enough to heal the sick and release the captives.

This book draws its materials from the voluminous files of the Rev. Roland J. Brown, who at this writing is pastor of the Parkside Baptist Church, Chicago.

It was here at his home where I interviewed him in regard to his healing work. I was with him a week. When I left I had little doubt but that the Rev. Mr. Brown possessed one of the largest collections of religious experience now in existence. There are larger collections of course, which have been gathered from many sources. The Pastor Brown collection has the distinction of being exclusively his own, however, for every case in his file is the result of his own personal intercession and ministry.

The selections made for this book are chiefly in the department of physical and mental healing, although the Pastor's prayer experiences cover a wide range of other problems involving human relationships, family, industrial, and the like, as well as experiences of personality and character as related to the redemptive processes of God.

Many of the cases included here are of a rather startling nature, as the reader will discover. Some of them may even tax the capacity to believe or the power to accept. But all are true. Here will be found a large number of the so-called incurable diseases, such as cancer, coronary thrombosis, alcoholism, dementia praecox, epilepsy, paralysis, gangrene, and others.

The book will reveal clinical prayer at its best, I am

sure. Each case will show something of a methodical treatment, and will thus serve as an excellent guide book for other ministers who may be interested in a similar ministry.

The Rev. Roland J. Brown is a theologian and a scholar, having also majored in psychology. He is a man of deep faith and rare compassion, ever ready to sacrifice personal comfort in the discharge of his mission. Faith and compassion and his willingness to serve all people regardless of class, creed, or race, is perhaps, the main secret of his success. He works under the guidance of the Spirit, and willingly submits to those disciplines which make men sensitive to and receptive of the divine powers. He is, in a word, a free and open instrument for the flow of healing currents, and he holds that any minister can likewise be effective in clinical prayer, if he is obedient to the commandments of Love.

The Rev. Mr. Brown is a splendid teacher of theology, and he is an eloquent and convincing speaker. I managed to persuade him that he had too long delayed in sharing the third empire of his ministry, that of healing, with a sick and fitful world. He was hesitant about this, as anyone might well be. Yet, I pleaded that it was surely the desire of Jesus to spread "good news" and that healing was very good news indeed, considering the state of humanity today. If a minister had this gift he should not refuse to admit it because of timidity or the fear of adverse criticism. He should not hide his light under a basket, or in any way attempt to conceal the good fruits of faith and Love.

Still he is not to be blamed for his reluctance. The field of spiritual healing has been crowded with a curious assortment of so-called "healers" who prey upon the desperation of the sick, always claiming much and producing little. In this way the healing ministry has been hurt. Probably many ministers have the healing gift, and refuse to exercise it because of the danger to their reputations.

And many, no doubt, have lost the gift because of negligence. If a man fails to use a talent "even that which he hath shall be taken away." It is always dangerous to a nice reputation to follow Him who bestows a new life.

On the other hand, many ministers may take their directions from the Apostle Paul rather than from Jesus. If it be preaching then tend to preaching. If it be healing then tend to healing. If it be teaching then tend to teaching. If it be prophecy then tend to prophesying. But by precept and example Jesus commissions his ministers to preach and teach and heal.

The Rev. Mr. Brown has taken his orders from Jesus. He specializes not in one gift but in three. Whether he has made a success of the healing gift the reader may judge after reading this book.

As a final comment on the man, let me say that he is known to his Chicago flock as Pastor Brown. It is a title of endearment and appreciation. We shall use the title as our tribute to the man who has done so much for so many.

The Pastor joins me in sending the book forth, not as a volume of sensation, but as a document of answered prayer, as a testimony to God's power, and as a missionary of hope to the ill: as "good news" revealing the abundant, victorious life. The book may fall short on the literary side; but as a living witness it cannot fail.

STARR DAILY

San Gabriel, Calif.
1948

Chapter I . . . . . .

Lost In Astonishment

"Cancer Can Be Cured"

"LUCREZIA GRAZZI had a cancer in one of her breasts," writes P. J. Bacci in his *Life of St. Philip Neri,* "and the physician had determined to apply the hot iron to it, and ordered her to remain in bed for the operation. She, however, in the meanwhile, moved with faith in her holy father, betook herself to St. Philip Neri and related her case to him. Philip answered, 'Oh, my poor child, where is this cancer?' She pointed to it, saying, 'Here, my Father.' Then the Saint, touching the diseased part, added, 'Go in peace and doubt not that you shall recover.' When she was come home, she said to those who were present, 'I feel neither pain nor oppression, and I firmly believe I am cured,' and so it proved to be. Soon after the physicians came to cauterize the cancer, and were lost in astonishment at finding not a trace of the disease."

Are cures like this limited to the Middle Ages? Or, to the time of Christ? Dr. Alexis Carrel, Nobel Prize Winner of the Rockefeller Foundation of Medical Research, does not think so. In his famous volume, *Man the Unknown,* he places himself on record as having actually *seen* the cancerous tissue made new while someone was in the process of prayer.

If we would seek confirmation of this type of miracle

from someone who actually did the praying we should consult Reverend Roland Brown.

"A member of your church is going to die of cancer," he was told, "will you come and pray with him?"

"Are you sure it is cancer?" he asked.

"Yes, for a long time he kept feeling pain in the region of his bladder. An examination was made, a sample of the tissue was removed and microscopically observed, and the verdict is unmistakable. His family wish you would come and see him."

"I found him sitting in the living room of his home," said Pastor Brown. "His loved ones were gathered about him. All were faithful followers of the Great Physician. I stood directly behind the patient's chair, my hands upon his head. I felt a saturation point of Love within myself, which became an outpouring through my hands to the afflicted man. I was caught up, as it seemed, in a contagion of holy affection for him, and it was as though this energy of Love escaped from the very pores of my body. I prayed for the man in an unmodified state of authority and conviction. Without the slightest hesitation or doubt I asked for a complete healing of the cancer, even as I prayed for the emancipation of his soul."

"What was the result?" I asked.

"We all thank God," replied the Pastor, "our friend has not suffered from the effects of cancer since that seemingly fatal hour."

In the briefest possible words this states the case of one Bill Eierman of Chicago, a member of Pastor Brown's Parkside Baptist Church. Whether we can understand it or not the case is on file, the diagnosis is a matter of record. It seems like a miracle, since cancer cannot be simulated or hysterically produced. But how can the affected cells be reactivated by Love and prayer, and the diseased tissue made new? The writer has no answer to that *how*. It is done by life, and by an Intelligence within life. Of this there can be no doubt. Somehow this Intelligence within life can be contacted by means of Love and faith, or perhaps by some supersensitive instinct.

There was still another case of cancer healing in the file of Pastor Brown where he was not even present when the healing took place. In this instance the following scripture was quite apt: "He sent his word and healed them, and delivered them from their destruction."

Explained the Pastor: "While conducting a prayer meeting at the Camp Farthest Out in Minnesota, 1942, Mrs. Ethel Wedemeier requested prayer for a close relative who had cancer of the throat. We all agreed that God was able to heal the disease, and in our fellowship of Love and faith we asked the Divine Physician to touch the suffering man and impart the necessary virtue to him. We then proceeded to drop the matter, leaving the patient with God, while we took up other requests. In that moment the healing process was set in motion. The man recovered rapidly, and to this day has remained in excellent health."

How was this cancerous tissue reformed by Love and prayer across many miles of intervening space? We do not know. We only know that such seemingly miraculous reforms can be accomplished by life and intelligence. As for bridging space with Love and prayer we may quote from *Man Does Not Stand Alone*:

"A female moth placed in your attic by the open window will send out some subtle signal. Over an unbelievable area, the male moths of the same species will catch the message and respond in spite of your attempts to produce laboratory odors to disconcert them. Has the little creature a broadcasting station, and has the male moth a mental radio set beside his antennae? Does she shake the ether and does he catch the vibration? The katydid rubs its legs or wings together, and on a still night can be heard half a mile away. It shakes six hundred tons of air and calls its mate."

If such lowly creatures as insects find no difficulty in bridging space then why should we be surprised when the prayers of men reach across the miles?

This book will be crowded with astonishing recoveries. In our present state of scientific and spiritual development we shall not understand how a minister of Love and faith can do these things; but, as he puts it, God does them through him, and his files are available, a stock pile of evidence in support of every claim. In this book we have a document of answered prayer. It is not fiction. It is fact.

"Can anybody exercise this gift of healing?" I asked Pastor Brown.

"Anybody who will expose himself to and pay the price for the Love of God can have a ministry of healing. With Love all things are possible."

Everywhere people are asking: "But what do you mean when you speak of Love? Is it an emotional power? a mental power? a spiritual power? or what is it?"

In Pastor Brown it is emotional. He feels an outgoing Love for those in distress who seek his aid. But as someone has said, "You cannot command a feeling." That is true. Then if one cannot command the feeling of Love, and if Love is necessary in the healing ministry, such as he pursues, how can anybody exercise the healing gift?

My own conviction is that the seat of holy affection is in the personal will. Feeling is a result, a manifestation of Love. But before it is feeling it is a mental process, that of exercising goodwill and peace toward others. Peaceful, patient attitudes and goodwill can be commanded. The price spoken of is eternal vigilance and heroic self-discipline. These attitudes and disciplines expose one to the Love of God which manifests as a corresponding emotion.

At the birth of Jesus the healing process was announced as peace on earth, good-will toward men. We can act peacefully and we can command good-will. May I illustrate the point out of a personal experience?

Some years ago I was seeking to aid a man who had been in prison. After investing nearly a thousand dollars in him he laughed at my guilelessness and let me know in plain language that he had had no other intention but to take advantage of me. My reaction to this was negative, that of ill-will. I had no feeling of Love for him. Nor could I arbitrarily command such a feeling into existence. But I did have the power to command my will. I could exercise peace and patience and good-will toward him. Instead of a mental reaction against him, I could mentally respond to God for him. I mentally detached myself from my loss of money. I sought divine forgiveness for being a temptation and stumblingblock to the man, a contributor to his weakness rather than his strength. By this process of reason and prayer and good-will there came a day when I was flooded with the emotion of Love, an experience worth more than all the wealth of the world.

And there came a day when the man sought me with a desire to reform his old attitude and position. I responded with further material assistance and a perfect sense of confidence. He voluntarily began to repay, and his first payment was fifty cents. His healing was gradual and in the end most thorough and beautiful.

There are people we cannot emotionally Love in the beginning. It is difficult to Love a fool or a tactless, blundering dolt. But we can express good-will toward him, and by and by this discipline will open our hearts to a corresponding emotion, and we shall Love him, even as Jesus Loved the foolish, tactless, blundering Peter, and our Love will heal the dolt as did the Love of Jesus heal the doltish disciple in the end.

We cannot muster up the emotion of Love for a self-deceived bore, or for a person who drops in at the most ungodly times, and who remains an hour after rising to leave. But as we stand there shifting our weight from leg to leg we can command good-will toward our visitor, and we can respond to God for him instead of reacting bitterly against him.

There are some neighbors we cannot Love emotionally. But we can command our wills to be good toward them, and we can pray that they become what they ought to be. We cannot Love ourselves all the time in a high, fine way. But we can exercise good-will toward ourselves, and pray to become what we should Love to become—a real man or woman.

"With Love all things are possible." This statement may constitute one of the primary dogmas in the healing ministry of Pastor Brown. We shall now present a case in support of the statement. If ever there existed a seemingly impossible and hopeless situation it will be found here. Literally Love in this case turned the certain victory of death into the glowing victory of life.

Chapter II . . . . . .

Compassion Has Its Inning

"Gangrene Goes"

"THE MAN was dying," said Pastor Brown, "of gangrene infection. When I visited him in the Cook County Hospital, Chicago, the attending doctors had given him less than twenty-four hours to live, for the poison was spreading rapidly."

The patient was a total stranger to the Pastor. Intercession had been sought for him by his mother-in-law. He was located in a small room apart from the main ward. This room was reserved for those who were about to die, in order to protect other ward patients from the damaging psychological effects of death. As the Pastor approached the patient's bed the man was shaking violently —so much so that the bed itself was agitated.

"He was a robust fellow," Pastor Brown went on, "the father of three children. This was a splendid fact for me to learn."

"Why?" I asked.

"It awakened in me a lively compassion for the waiting family; and stirred a sense of urgency for the father to be well and back home."

"You consider the compassion an indispensable factor, then?"

"In the healing ministry of Jesus how often it is reported, 'He had compassion upon them!' Oh, yes, Love is an essential power."

With this he returned to the case at hand. "The man feared he might lose his leg. He seemed unaware that he was losing his life. He told me that he was shaking because he had not taken morphine all day. For seven days and nights he had been drugged on morphine in order to endure his pain. During that time there had been no natural sleep. Nor had a bite of food been taken through the mouth. The day I came he had refused the drug for the first time, though he had not known of my coming. This fact also had a good effect upon me, giving me what seemed to be a sense of destiny in my visit. I then asked him if he believed in the power of prayer. He told me that he did. And I therefore sought to assure him that we could pray with confidence."

And so the Pastor began his clinical petition. He prayed a long time in the hope of calming the man's mind and body. But nothing of the sort took place. He stopped praying. Under a new inspiration he asked the patient, "Are you a Christian?" The man, without hesitation, replied that he was. The Pastor was a little baffled at this prompt affirmation. He pressed the point: "Have you accepted Jesus Christ as your personal Savior? Your Redeemer?" The patient looked up at him in wonderment. "Why, I guess I don't know exactly what you mean, Mr. Brown."

The Pastor began to instruct the man in the Christian faith. He was told of the substitutionary atonement of Jesus upon the Cross, and how the Lord had taken upon himself the sins of the world. Though he was incapable of understanding a doctrine so deep and involved as vicarious atonement, he nevertheless listened with a simple, childlike faith. He was moved by the thought that men could be forgiven, their bodies healed and their souls released by the Master's wonderful Love and Grace. The man's eyes grew moist, and then tears came which caused him embarrassment. He thought they were a display of weakness, and attempted an apology, which the Pastor interrupted.

"Never be ashamed of this kind of feeling," he said. "I'm glad for your tears. They show the cleansing work of the Holy Spirit, which is going on in your soul at this very moment. Though you may not have deeply accepted the Lord Jesus you do believe in him and now accept him as your Savior, don't you?"

The man replied with a choked voice, "Yes, oh yes, I do."

Said Pastor Brown: "I looked at him now with joy in my heart, and as I gazed down at him his shaking ceased for the first time. My joy was again loosed when he said: 'Oh, I feel so much better. You know, I believe I could eat something.' And I replied, 'Yes, you will be able to eat.' He then told me that he was feeling drowsy and thought he could go to sleep. I said to him: 'Yes. You're going to sleep. You're going to have a supernatural sleep. Not in the claws of morphine; but in the loving, healing arms of Jesus. When you wake you'll be hungry. And you'll eat.' Already his lids were heavy and closing as he lay there perfectly still."

Let me remind the reader at this point not only of the doctrine which Pastor Brown employed but of the authority he used to reassure the patient: "You're going to have a supernatural sleep. You'll wake and be able to eat. You'll sleep in the loving, healing arms of Jesus."

When there is Love and faith present in the practitioner there also seems to be this sense of authority and boldness in the Spirit to give firm, positive reassurance to the sufferer. We saw this in St. Philip Neri as he treated the cancer case in the previous chapter: "Then the Saint, touching the diseased part, added, 'Go in peace and doubt not that you shall recover.' " In a tumor problem treated by St. Philip we find him again speaking in the boldness of spiritual authority and firm reassurance: "There, my child, don't be afraid. You won't be troubled with it any more. It will soon be well." And the woman forthwith recovered.

In the light of modern psychological knowledge it would be difficult to improve upon St. Philip's treatment. While the psychotherapist of today employs the method of reassurance, he is likely to do so in a limited way. The sense of Divine Authority is missing in his suggestive approach. In the absence of holy affection for the patient he hesitates to affirm, "You will be healed." It is this boldness in the Spirit which gives Pastor Brown his power in the use of assurance. But to the outcome.

Said the Pastor: "In a few minutes the man was lost to suffering. The needed natural slumber had come. God could now work unhampered."

When next Pastor Brown visited the patient he had been returned to the ward, having been moved the day following his first call. The man was sitting up in bed, a smile on his face. He exclaimed:

"Oh, I'm so glad to see you, Mr. Brown. For I want to tell you they'll not have to amputate my leg. I thanked the doctors. But they told me not to thank them, for they had had nothing to do with it. It seemed like a miracle to them, Mr. Brown."

He then showed Pastor Brown his leg. It had been black from foot to knee. Now only the big toe was discolored. The Pastor prayed again for a total recovery. When next he came to the hospital all the poison was gone. The man was soon reunited with his wife and children.

From a medical point of view this afflicted man was the same as dead. From Love's point of view his affliction was God's opportunity to reveal His power and set forth a witness to His Glory.

Many ministers have the gifts of Love and faith, and

also the counselling gift of reassurance. Yet they hesitate to use their talents to relieve suffering. Many are prevented because of inhibiting clauses in doctrine. Some may not even be aware that they are instruments of Love and faith and healing. But those who are capable of Love and faith are healers whether they exercise the gift or not. They have a strong influence over the negative conditions which oppress and distress their people.

In this connection will you, the reader, try to imagine yourself in the following situation. For twenty-five years you have been handicapped, tormented, and vexed with a weak, unreliable heart. You have been often warned to take it easy, to avoid the slightest excitement and strain. You have been unable to plan ahead for a vacation, or for anything that would alter the easy-going program of your daily life. Over you has hung the disagreeable feeling of being an invalid, a burden to others, or an object of pity, perhaps, and charity. Always echoing in your mind has been the grim commandment: "Thou shalt not. Be careful. Watch yourself. Don't overdo."

Try to conceive just what such a life of constant precaution would be like if it were yours to endure. Think of the bleak, hopeless verdict of medical science as reported through your doctor, "Nothing can be done to cure you."

That was the life of Mrs. Lee for a quarter of a century. Over against this fatal verdict stood Pastor Brown, armed with Love and faith. When you have followed her case through the next chapter you too may be inclined to say, "Surely with Love and faith *all* things are possible."

Chapter III . . . . .

A Heart Made Whole

"A Cardiac Condition Healed"

"IN twenty-five long, weary years," said Pastor Brown, "there had never been a week for Mrs. Lee that was free from the necessity of remaining in bed one whole day. In her work, her play, her social life, her church interests, she had been greatly limited.

"There came the day when she was ordered by her doctor to give up all activity and to remain at home to conserve her ebbing strength. She was to settle down to the dull, monotonous routine of the hopeless, confirmed invalid. Just waiting for the end!"

It was at this crucial point that Pastor Brown came in to disturb the prescribed destiny. He brought in an atmosphere of assurance. The best medical treatment had delayed the crisis, had kept the patient limping along. But now the Jericho Walls of science had been hammered down in a crumbled heap of disappointment. Across the medical chart of this woman's life had been written the hard, sullen word of "Failure." The case was closed. The climax of her life was now in sight.

The Pastor, in the face of this verdict from the bench of science, felt his heart declaring "No" in the unmistakable language of an outpouring Love and a rising state of faith. Under the impact of this Love and faith he experienced the guiding intelligence of the Spirit. His approach to the patient was prompt and unhesitating. Immediately he launched a psychotherapeutic program. This took the usual form of stimulating reassurance. The Pastor's genial manner, his certainty, his Love, the quiet and quieting tonal quality of his voice—these were his initial instruments. To reinforce them and implement their effectiveness he began to do something specific and concrete.

"You are to relax," he told the patient. And with this he gave her careful instructions, a series of exercises calculated to render her passive to God in body, mind, and soul. He then began prayer therapy. His voice was soft, his manner confident. His accents were sonorous and clear. His vocal prayer was like music, hymn music. As he continued in prayer his eyes were closed, his Love glowed and his faith grew.

"When I had finished praying," he said, "Mrs. Lee was limp. She had sunk into a deep and healing experience of Union with Christ. By means of this three-way yielding to God's Love, body, mind, and soul, she received recovery in body, mind, and soul."

The Pastor was urged to go on. "Then what happened?"

His eyes were filled with an unearthly light. All the radiance of his grateful soul was burning in their gray depths as he replied:

"For many days after this Mrs. Lee went about her duties as one living in a new and glorified world. She had touched Centre and had come forth a brand-new creature in Christ Jesus, the old things having passed away as if by some inconceivable magic. Her cross had been shouldered by the Master. He had rolled away the stone from her door of death. She herself phrased it as walking on light air, where before she had dragged herself about in the turgid waters of a sluggish stream. For many years the cardiograms had revealed an incurable condition of the heart. When her physician noted the change in her he was surprised and immediately made a new cardiogram. And to his astonishment it showed Mrs. Lee as completely healed. The doctor was frank and honest. He told Mrs. Lee that her recovery was nothing less than miraculous in the light of orthodox medical knowledge."

This recovery was attained by a method of psychological reassurance, plus the authority of Love and trust in God. The Pastor passes over from the mental application to the spiritual source of power with an ease that is sometimes startling. The purely scientific therapist lacks this freedom of range, so that when he effects a cure he attributes it to the mind of the patient, even as the medical doctor attributes it to nature. But the genuine spiritual therapist follows the Jesus example and attributes the cure to God. "Not mine but Thine is the power." "Of myself I can do nothing." "The Father He doeth the works." And so on. The credit being placed where the credit is due!

It may be helpful at this place to report a healing of Mrs. Lee's son. One cannot say for certain, but the mother's experience may have had a stimulating effect on the boy's faith. Having been healed herself by what was apparently an extra-natural power, and having her own faith thus enriched, she may have transmitted something of this to her young son. At any rate, the boy, too, in a physical emergency was healed through prayer and the touch method. Said Pastor Brown:

"William Lee's ear was aching severely. It had been troubling him for some time. He didn't know the cause of it. Nor did his mother. But now it was certain that unless something was done soon the boy would have to have medical treatment. At this time the pain was intense. In spite of his agony, however, he wanted to participate in our evening church service. So he came. I took the boy to an upper room, put my hands over his ears, allowed my Love to bathe him, and in faith asked God to remove his pain. While I was still in silent prayer William said, 'I feel something going pop in my ear.' And instantly the pain was gone and he experienced no further trouble. When he reached home after the service he was excited. He could hardly wait to relate what God had done for him. As a result William's faith in God to heal has been wonderfully enlivened."

As I ponder these two remarkable healings there comes a reminder of something Jesus said to all future ministers: "Verily, verily, I say unto you; he that believeth on me, the works that I do shall he do also." This is a difficult promise for most ministers to accept. It seems too good to be true. The Pastor took it literally. For many years, moved by the distresses of the members of his church, he prayed for the gifts of Love and faith and healing, and submitted himself to those austere spiritual habits of constant prayer and meditation which seem so necessary in the life of the spiritual therapist.

It is surely an awesome thing to possess the gift of healing, unless perhaps one is strong enough to balance capability against responsibility. The temptation to abuse such power must at times be overwhelming, even though it be known that the misuse of it can lead only to a grave disaster.

There is in my memory a number of persons who at one time in their lives possessed the gift to heal, and by its exercise were able to help many get release from their misfortunes. But having commercialized and otherwise abused their talent they lost it. With the loss came tragedy. For now they continued to pretend what they no longer owned. On the strength of their past reputation suffering people kept coming to them, only to be disillusioned ultimately in all spiritual therapists and even in God Himself.

It is, in fact, chiefly because of the commercial exploitation of a gift that no longer exists that healing through prayer has come into such disrepute among thinking people and more especially among those of the medical profession. The persons who practice a pretense for gain and self-exaltation must of course pay the price for their hypocrisy, and the price is often spiritual suicide.

It may be that many Christian ministers shy away from healing because the field has been so hurt and exploited by counterfeit "healers." They do not like to expose their reputations for clear thinking to the dangers of such a ministry, and especially to the temptations which go with healing power. The line between a Satanic practice and a genuine Christian doctrine is often so fine as to be unrecognizable. "Fools leap in where angels fear to tread, and the very elect of God may be deceived." The Enemy himself will put the name of Jesus upon the lips of his unwitting servants. These are days when glamour tempts and glory repels, when the pagan hearts will be made to blaspheme and cry "Lord, Lord." We can hardly blame the Christian minister who turns from his Lord's commission to heal the sick. Millions are eagerly in pursuit of the gifts, and only a few are willing to pay the cost for the Giver.

Once a man is exposed to and possessed by that Giver the gifts externalize themselves in wonderful and mysterious ways. The originality of the Spirit's method is often as astounding as His results. The reader is about to witness an amazing evidence of this in the case of Don Lonchar. The title of the following chapter could well be, "Recovery By Spiritual Heat."

Chapter IV . . . . .

The Healing Touch

"A Lieutenant Healed"

AS AN interviewer as well as an observer and student eager to learn, my days with Pastor Brown were personally fruitful. He always spoke much of the ministry of the Spirit. From what he said and by what he has done in his healing work, two conclusions have been crystallized in my thought.

First, when under the inspiration and guidance of the Spirit, there is an originality of method. Second, when in the power of the Spirit there is an originality of experience.

In my study of the cases treated in this book I perceive that Pastor Brown rarely if ever employed the same method. His approach to different people was made differently. According to their faith, and conditioned by their temperament, it was done unto them. I have noted this same capacity for originality in the lives of others who exercised the healing gift.

Thomas of Celano, in his *Lives Of St. Francis Of Assisi,* reports a case of paralysis after this fashion: "Once when the man of God had come to Narni and was staying there several days, a man of that city named Peter was lying in bed paralyzed. For five months he had been so completely deprived of the use of all his limbs that he could in no wise lift himself up or move at all; and thus having lost all help from feet, hands, and head, he could only move his tongue and open his eyes. But on hearing that St. Francis was come to Narni, he sent a messenger to the Bishop to ask that he would, for Divine Compassion's sake, be pleased to send the servant of God Most High to him, for he trusted that he would be delivered by the sight and presence of the Saint from the infirmity whereby he was holden, and so indeed it came to pass; for when the blessed Francis was come to him *he made the sign of the cross over him from head to feet* (the italics are mine), and forthwith drove away all his sickness and restored him to his former health."

Here there was apparently no need for words in the method of St. Francis: only a need for motion, a describing with his hand the sign of a cross. In this same connection another case is reported:

"There was a brother who often suffered from a grievous infirmity that was horrible to see. Oftentimes he was dashed down, and with a terrible look in his eyes he wallowed foaming; sometimes his limbs were contracted, sometimes extended, sometimes they were folded and twisted together, and sometimes they became hard and rigid. Sometimes, tense and rigid all over, with his feet touching his head, he would be lifted up in the air to the height of a man's stature and would then suddenly spring back to earth. The holy father, Francis, pitying his grievous sickness, went to him, and *after offering up prayer,* signed him with the red cross, *and blessed him.* And suddenly he was made whole, and never afterwards suffered from this distressing infirmity." (Italics mine.)

In this second case the method was similar but different. Here the patient was touched, vocal prayer was employed, and finally a verbal blessing was uttered. The results in both cases were the same, non original. Each man was made whole, was healed. But the experience of being healed was different with each man, and the method of healing was also different.

No two spiritual experiences can ever be precisely the same. God honors man's individuality, approaches each man differently according to his faith, and each man's experience of God's Love and grace must of necessity be original, for no two men have been created alike. All men are similar; but each bears the stamp of the Creator's originality.

In my two former books, *Release,* and *Love Can Open Prison Doors,* I have described my own transforming experience. Comparing it with others I find a similarity but an originality. After publishing these books the opportunity came to found a religious movement. The opportunity was also a temptation. If such a movement would have inspired people to yield and work out their own salvation it would have been justified. If, on the other hand, it would have wooed people into a state of personal apathy, so that they were willing to rest upon and be content with my experience, instead of inviting an original experience of their own, then my experience would have become a stumbling block. Each denomination was organized around some one's original spiritual experience. Denominations become dangerous, therefore, when people become content with them. If they offer an escape from the demands of original experience they can surely work against the purpose of God which is emancipation of each soul, not by a stereotype, mass production line method, but by a method as original as the individual involved. One of the distinctive marks of Jesus' approach is this self-same originality and the honoring of it in the individuals he treated. Often he healed persons in the way they wished to be healed.

And so in Pastor Brown and his healing ministry I have observed the originality of the Spirit in method and experience. The methods employed as instruments of the

Spirit are original, and the manifestations of the Spirit's power are original. In the case of Don Lonchar there is something not far removed in application from the heat therapy now being used by medical doctors. The resemblance is quite marked, as you will see. Yet the originality in its operation is unmistakable.

Don was a young man of faith. He felt that during the war he had experienced answered prayer. While he was a lieutenant in the Air Force, his plane was shot down one day near Eniwetok, and he found himself struggling in the ocean with a wounded arm. He possessed but half his life belt, and he had never learned to swim. For an hour he managed to keep afloat, and was finally rescued. He was convinced that his faith and prayer had prevented his drowning. Months later when he had come home and was on terminal leave, while crossing a street in Chicago, he was knocked down by an automobile. He was rushed to the General Hospital. A week passed and he was still unable to move his right leg. It was the opinion of the doctors that a nerve near the hip joint had been injured with the possibility that the young man would remain partially paralyzed.

Now if Pastor Brown could establish union with Jesus through the means of faith and prayer; if he could fully realize in his heart that Jesus in turn had an unbroken union with the Father; and finally if Don also could be identified through faith with this union, a healing no doubt would be effected.

So when it all appeared dark for the lad, with a long period in the hospital promised, the Pastor said to him: "Suppose we talk to God about this, Don? Suppose we ask the Holy Spirit to burn out anything that should not be in you, that you may be completely healed."

Here is the method of subtle persuasion at work.

Don responded to it. It brought to his remembrance former answers to prayer. Clear as a beacon stood out his rescue from the waves of the Pacific Ocean. He was stirred with new hope. His faith rose to the Pastor's suggestion as a fish to the fly.

Pastor Brown then brought in the method of touch. He put his palm on the injured part. He prayed with a deep sense of trust, asking the Holy Spirit to take charge through him and heal Don.

Cooperation in prayer was now sought by the Pastor, not only for Don's physical healing, but for a redemptive experience. At the conclusion of this formal prayer they held a period of conversational prayer, while Pastor Brown kept his hand on the injured leg. By and by Don asked, "Is it unusually warm in here, Pastor?" And the reply was. "No. It feels comfortable to me."

It was not so with Don, however. He declared that he was burning up. He opened his bed robe and shook it in an effort to get relief from the terrific heat. His pajamas were soaked as though they had been dipped in water. The lad was perspiring all over, an experience such as he had never known.

"I felt his pajamas," said Pastor Brown, "and found them wringing wet. I reminded Don that we had asked the Spirit to burn out all the negative conditions, and that He evidently intended to do a good job of it. To this fact Don agreed." The Pastor went on:

"The following day I called on Don again. He was thrilled when I entered the room. 'Look, Pastor!' He drew his knee up to his chest, and then pushed the leg back. The day before he had been unable to move the member. He then swung himself around to the edge of the bed and stood up. He walked. Within a few days he was discharged from the hospital, feeling good, but showing a slight limp. Within a few more days the limp was gone. He was completely recovered, and to this day he has no doubt as to the Source of his blessing."

The Holy Spirit as He manifests is sometimes described

as a purging, redeeming fire, which not only heals infection in the body, but purifies the mind and heart and ego, thus healing the more subtle infections of the personality and character. This fire ministers to different people in different ways. With Don Lonchar it operated as a therapeutic heat, similar to the artificial fever produced by medical doctors.

It is perhaps probable that every normal person may exercise the gift of healing. This is because every normal person can make of himself an instrument of Christian Love. Every normal person has the power to express good-will toward others, and good-will is always good news. All that is needed is a disciplined mind and an open heart that is empty of self and filled with God's Love.

Some years ago while I was on a speaking tour a minister invited me to visit one of his flock, a young man who was afflicted with a disease for which medicine had no remedy. The minister had made up his mind to pray for this friend's recovery. It was a bold and dangerous step for him to take. The gift of healing had long been rejected in his church by previous pastors, so that the congregation were dead set against this "modern magic."

As we rode along he said: "If this man gets well, and it gets out that I prayed for his healing, I'll be persecuted by the members and officers in my church. They'll do anything for the fellow, make any personal sacrifice, but to pray for his healing would be little less than apostasy."

I thought that was a curious attitude for a follower of the Great Physician. But I said nothing against it, not knowing the evidence they had to support it. I was glad that the minister was going to fly into the teeth of it, however, stand upon his honor and integrity, and do what he felt to be the Christian thing in spite of the danger to his popular reputation. "This is my commandment, That ye Love one another."

Surely that is Christian. And this Love turns theological opinion into nothingness, as the light of truth dispels the darkness of falsehood. Love wants people to be well whether or not they ever get well. Imagine a mother or father who would refuse to pray for a suffering child! Such coldness would be abnormal. And he who really Loves Jesus and who Loves as Jesus Loved will do all he can to help people, including a recourse to prayer.

Christians who do not Love may teach and preach. Those who do Love may also heal. And if they really Love they will heal regardless of outworn theological conclusions which stand out against them. There is only a little teaching and preaching which glorifies God. But no healing accomplished through His Love fails to glorify Him.

The Apostles Loved much and healed many. The very shadow of Peter healed people. Having God's Love in his heart he could not help healing. It was automatic. And people were healed by receiving items from Paul's apparel. One may ask, therefore, what has happened to the gift of Christian healing? Why has it been rejected?

Could it be that our ministers of today lack Love, the healing power? Truly if they are powerless they are living in exile to Christian Love. They may be eloquent, but if their eloquence has been gained in the absence of Love, as Paul puts it, they are empty, sounding brass and tinkling cymbals. Or as Dr. E. Stanley Jones has phrased it in effect, "They are verbal but not vital." When there is no Christian Love there can be no vitality. Only dead forms, tiresome rituals, and fruitless observances. Pastor Brown is a minister with Love, and Pastor Brown also has a ministry of healing. When you have finished with the following case you will marvel and be glad for his Love and healing power. Here let the psychiatrists draw up a chair.

Chapter V . . . .

A Demon Cast Out

"Schizophrenia Abdicates"

THIS chapter will deal with a common disease in an uncommon way. In our modern psychiatrical terminology one type of the mental break is called dementia praecox, or schizophrenia, a condition characterized by a split personality.

Back in the days of Jesus such persons were said to be possessed of demons or evil spirits. This diagnosis is disputed by the psychologists of today. They do not grant obsession in quite the same way, such as an invasion of one personality by the discarnate spirit of another. They do grant obsession of ideas, opinions, conclusions, fears, etc. Nor do the modern doctors agree with the treatment that was employed by Jesus and his early followers.

In the Gospel according to St. Mark, 16:15-18, Jesus instructs his disciples in the following words: "Go ye into all the world, and preach the gospel to every creature. . . . And these signs shall follow them that believe; In my name shall they cast out devils . . . they shall lay hands on the sick, and they shall recover."

Here, then, what we call dementia praecox or schizophrenia, is a mental affliction which, in the time of Jesus, was called "devil possession." In our day the disease is treated in hospitals, usually over long periods of time.

Some cures are obtained. In many cases the patients live and die in their affliction.

Jesus healed the unfortunate victims on the spot simply by "casting out the devils or demons" in them. His disciples were empowered to do likewise.

Whether dementia praecox is what the moderns say it is, or whether it is what Jesus said it was, will be a disputed question for a long time. So will the dispute rage between the two diametrically opposite types of treatment.

Now as we have seen, Pastor Brown majored in psychology. He is, therefore, familiar with the modern opinion and treatment. He is also a theologian, and is therefore familiar with the opinions and treatment of Jesus. This is important to know about the Pastor, for while he often employs modern psychiatrical methods, in the following extraordinary case, he used the Jesus method with prompt and astounding results. He took literally that part of the scripture just quoted: "And these signs shall follow them that believe; in my name shall they cast out devils."

Whether it was a devil which was cast out in the present instance, or whether it was a self-created and self-sustained fixation, is a rather shoddy dispute in view of the result, the freeing of an isolated and tormented personality.

The work of casting out devils was a major part of Jesus' healing ministry. His disciples were not always successful with mental cases because they were lacking in faith. Is this the reason why his present-day disciples are unsuccessful? Before we move into a description of the case at hand, let us reexamine one of the classic instances of Jesus (Matthew 17:14-20):

> "And when they were come to the multitude, there came to him a certain man, kneeling down to him, and saying, Lord, have mercy on my son: for he is lunatic, and sore vexed. . . . And I brought him to thy disciples, and they could not cure him.

"Then answered Jesus and said, O faithless and perverse generation, how long shall I be with you! How long shall I suffer you! Bring him hither to me.

"And Jesus rebuked the devil; and he departed out of him: and the child was cured from that very hour. Then came the disciples to Jesus apart and said, 'Why could not we cast him out?'

"And Jesus said unto them, Because of your unbelief: for verily I say unto you, If ye have faith as a grain of mustard seed, ye shall say unto this mountain, Remove hence to yonder place; and it shall remove; and nothing shall be impossible unto you."

He was talking directly to his faithless disciples when he accused them of being a "perverse generation" who had so little faith that they could not heal a mental affliction. In using the word *perverse* Jesus was actually indicting his ministers of being schizoid types themselves. The same indictment was against our modern psychiatrists who fail to heal these mental diseases. All are a perverse generation. A *perverse* personality is an antisocial type: one lacking in Christian Love and faith. In extreme cases he is psychopathic in his personality behavior. He is constitutionally inferior, with a tendency toward moral insanity. Thus while there are many degrees of perversity, the term "perverse" applies to everybody who is alien to the Love and direction of God. The only sane person is a God-empowered person. When this accusation is aimed at the ministers of God it is serious. They are not supposed to be schizoid types. They are supposed to be in union with God through faith, and therefore sane personalities. How can the vast mass of schizoids in the academic, cultural, scientific, business and professional world, and in all other departments of life, have any hope of being cured of perversity, if the ministers of God themselves are not cured? "Can Satan cast out Satan?" "Because of your unbelief." "O faithless and perverse generation."

Now if Pastor Brown can, by faith, heal an advanced case of schizophrenia, the same way Jesus healed such cases, he may be considered sane, a minister who does what Jesus tells him to do, and who has the faith necessary to do it. The results will determine his status and authority. "By their fruits ye shall know them."

For obvious reasons the name of the patient is withheld. He may be called Frank for convenience.

One day Pastor Brown received a letter from Dr. Glenn Clark, a man of faith and power in prayer. Dr. Clark was at this time a professor at Macalester College in St. Paul, Minnesota. He sought the Pastor's aid on behalf of Frank, suggesting that he visit the patient if he were ever in Minneapolis.

The Pastor went to that city in August, 1939. With Dr. Clark he paid Frank a visit. Frank was under the care of an excellent doctor. His case had been treated for years by the best psychiatrical science and sympathetic understanding, but without results. Everyone proclaimed him incurably insane.

Dr. Clark had been seeing Frank for two years, but the patient had never responded to prayer.

Frank was a personality casualty of the First World War. At the time of this event he was forty years of age. Twenty years before he had gone into war with ideals which were not compatible with the violence and horror of warfare. The break came. His was a beautiful soul in bondage to a terrified mind and disrupted nervous system. It was as though he were in the clutches of a merciless demon. And this control had lasted for twenty years. For ten years he had isolated himself in his room, refusing to venture forth from it even for a moment. For one year he had declined all entreaties and had remained in bed. He was growing steadily worse.

Dr. Clark and Pastor Brown sat by Frank's bed, the

Pastor remaining silent while the other two carried on a conversation. As Pastor Brown meditated upon Frank's plight, and on the sorrow of the aging parents, he felt a surge of compassion well up within him. His thoughts drifted away from the momentary scene and focused upon the historical Jesus, who wandered about the banks of Galilee with healing in his word and touch, casting out the devil afflictions of that day.

The Pastor found himself dwelling upon the promise Jesus made to his disciples. They too could cast out devils in his name. After Jesus had gone back to the Father they could do what he had done as he had promised them and even greater works would they do for the glory of God.

Thus returning in thought to the room, he was inspired with a new faith. He began to pray silently and specifically. He prayed that God would lift the veil from Frank's mind and blow away the fog from his bound soul. He prayed that Jesus would cast out any false ideas or misconceptions; that he would banish the evil spirits of delusion, fear, sin, and separation, even as he had discharged the demons of long ago.

Dr. Clark suddenly asked the patient a rather peculiar but apt question, "What would you say a demon is?"

"A demon is to be obsessed by a half truth," replied Frank.

"Can you illustrate what you mean?" asked Dr. Clark.

"Well, if a lion were caught in a butterfly net and thought he was a butterfly, he would be possessed by a demon."

That gave Dr. Clark the leverage he had been waiting for for two years. The prayers of Pastor Brown, sitting silently in the room, had helped to bring it to a focus. Now Dr. Clark prayed silently, "Heavenly Father, Frank has at last perfectly defined the demon that possesses him. Here he is a man who thinks he is a canary caught in a cage. For ten years he has remained in this room that he could easily have gotten out of any time he wished. In the name of Jesus Christ I command this demon to leave him and never return again."

"It appears that Frank was healed in that moment," said Pastor Brown. "The patient turned to me like a new person and asked me about myself, and wanted to know where I was going. There was interest in his words and an animation that was new to him. Where before he had seemed mechanical, now he was full of enthusiasm and interest. I told him I was on my way to the Camp Farthest Out, a religious conference, which had been founded by Dr. Clark several years ago. Frank's curiosity was aroused by this information. He wanted to know where the conference was and when it started. I told him it was at Lake Koronis and would begin the next day. He asked me what it was like, and I said it was like heaven on earth."

And with this statement Frank remarked quite suddenly, "I wish I could go there." To which the Pastor replied:

"Well, maybe you can. Why not?"

Then for the first time he asked a very practical question. "How much would it cost?"

This delighted Dr. Clark. He assured Frank that it could be arranged, and that he would take it up with his parents. When the latter were informed they were overjoyed at this unexpected sign of recovery. It was the first ray of hope they had seen in twenty sorrowful years.

On the second day of the conference Frank arrived, pale and perspiring, but victorious, his long years of bondage disputed and conquered. It seemed like a miracle to everyone. For Frank had been marvelously healed.

His triumph became the dynamic for the whole conference, an inspiration and stimulant to the faith of all.

That fall Frank became an active member of Dr. Clark's Bible class, where he served as receptionist, a kind of self-appointed host. He would stand at the door, smiling and courteous, greeting the people, eager always to serve their needs and make them feel welcome and at home. The Pastor summed up the case with a tribute:

"Today Frank's is one of the sweetest natures I've ever known. He is like that Israelite in whom there is no guile. Insincerity, expedience, dishonesty, untruthfulness are as foreign to his nature as hell is foreign to heaven. The vulgar scrutiny of the pretender is unknown to his innocent eye. His piety is not revealed by affectation. He wears no mask woven from the threads of religious sham and self-exaltation. In his character and deeds you see the wise and humble servant. To be with him for awhile is to hear your heart say, 'At last a clean man.' The artificial sophistication has disappeared. The fears and inferiorities, the perversities and delusions are gone. So are the dull hypocrisies of nominal and professional religion. Here is a man who nearly fits the Jesus standard as a candidate for the kingdom of heaven, 'Except ye turn and become as a little child ye shall in nowise enter; for of such is the kingdom of heaven.' I can pay no higher tribute to Frank than to say, 'Behold, a man.' For Frank, now free from the bondage of schizophrenia, offers his soul the temple of manhood."

This experience comes about as close to Jesus' method of healing the mentally sick as one can come, and yet nothing was done that was inconsistent with the highest discoveries of modern psychiatry. Perhaps the one chief difference is that it utilized a *plus* that psychiatry too rarely uses. While Dr. Clark had done the "spade work" for two years, the account of which would be a story in itself, the final creative step that led to the final cure, in the opinion of Dr. Clark, was the quiet prayer of Pastor Brown as he sat by the bedside filled with compassion and with irrepressible faith.

"The two chief factors in this cure," said Dr. Clark,

"might be summed up in two remarkable laws announced by Jesus. First: 'If two of you shall agree on earth as touching anything that they shall ask, it shall be done for them of My Father which is in heaven' (Matt. 18:19). Working alone I had not been able to pull Frank out of this, but with Pastor Brown whose faith in healing knows no limits there was an 'agreement' that could move mountains. Second: Whenever Jesus could discover the *names* of the demons, He was always able to command them. Modern psychiatrists follow the same general principle in their patient search to find the 'name' or 'cause' of the psychosis knowing that when that is discovered and commanded to leave, the patient recovers. Frank's defining the demon that was in him, furnished the handle by which it could be cast out forever."

A great physician has prophesied that there will be twelve million mental and nervous cases resulting from the second World War and the peak will come in 1956. Physicians and hospitals cannot carry the load. More and more they are looking for help to the clergy and to religious workers who believe that the time has come to take the teachings of Jesus out of the realm of theory and put them in the realm of practice.

The strains and stresses on the human mind and nervous system are growing rapidly while the department of healing lags far behind. To this end, and out of this necessity, psychosomatic medicine has come into being and is attracting practitioners in all the orbits of healing. Ministers especially are realizing more and more that they ought to be equipped to cope with mental and physical diseases among their own congregations. Some of them are even making a specialty of healing.

Of these the work of Dr. John Gaynor Banks, an Episcopal minister of San Diego, California, is outstanding. So imperative does he feel the need of a return to healing among the clergy to be that he has given up his church temporarily to devote his whole time and talent to this new interest. He has conducted healing missions in churches all over the United States, calling the sick to the altar and the ministers to the healing ministry. He is a skilled and penetrating writer in this field. His studies in Pastoral Psychology are sound, scientific, learned and practical, and his magazine, *Sharing,* is outstanding in the field of spiritual therapy.

In the years that are to come, hundreds of consecrated, Christ-like clergymen are going to follow in the footsteps of Dr. Banks and Pastor Brown and enlarge their Christian service to include the ministry of healing. "Come out from among the hesitant, timid, and unbelieving," they can hear the voice of Christ calling. *"Go ye into all the world and preach the gospel to every creature. . . . And these signs shall follow them that believe; in my name shall they cast out devils . . . . they shall lay hands on the sick, and they shall recover."*

Chapter VI . . . . .

Madness At The Altar

"Where Sympathy Brought Sanity"

IN THE preceding chapter you may have marveled at a case of split personality, thoroughly conditioned by twenty years of isolation and antisocial habits, which in the twinkle of an eye, was cured. Not only was the personality healed, but the soul was set free to find union with its Maker.

But still more astonishing, and far more dramatic, is the following case, this time a woman, who suffered a severe mental break while Pastor Brown was preaching a Sunday morning sermon. His handling of this delicate and explosive situation will grip you, and the outcome will leave you more convinced of a God who cares and who is able to do exceedingly abundantly for those who call upon Him in trust and unqualified confidence.

As I meditate upon the power of spiritual love, in the light of what happened in the life of this woman, a scripture which baffled me for years keeps coming into my mind: "The works that I do shall ye do also, and greater works than these shall ye do, because I go to the Father."

Perhaps every student of Jesus has puzzled over this promise. How could any man do greater works than those recorded in the New Testament? Who today could walk as he did on the water? Who, by uttering a brief command, could quiet a raging sea and still a storm? Who among us in this hour could perform greater works than these?

"Because I go to the Father, greater works than these shall ye do." That clause, "Because I go to the Father," holds the secret.

Because he has gone to the Father his Spirit has been made available to us. Only in the power of his Spirit can we do greater works. But we ask, "What greater works, for instance?"

Greater than walking upon the water is the healing of a sick mind, the purging of an evil heart, the shattering of a rebellious ego, until it bows in subjection to God's Will. Greater than commanding the elements is the quickening of a static spirit, the loosing of an earthbound soul, the changing of a personality and character.

As you read this chapter don't make the mistake of believing that promise, "Greater things shall ye do," is exclusive to the Pastor Browns of the earth. If someone tells you that such power is for a chosen few "don't you believe it." Any man can be "chosen" when he chooses to let God choose him, when he yields to God and meets the requirements of Love. The door is always open. "Whosoever will may come."

It is true that there are many things you cannot do. You cannot find God by striving and struggling. You cannot think your way into union with God nor obtain His power by self-effort and selfish motives. You cannot attain to God by seeking to possess Him. You cannot enter the Light on the wings of your ego, nor make the new wine flow into your old bottle.

It is equally true that there are many things you can do. You can yield to God's Will. He will empower you when you are ready and willing to let go and be empowered, and when you can Love as He would have you love.

Not by developing your personal will but by submitting it; not by struggling for self-improvement and self-attainment but by committing the self—these are the requirements of Him Who bestows the power. Yes, greater works can we do, now that he has gone to the Father, and has made his Spirit available to us, if and when we wish to accept the offering and pay the price, ourselves for His Self, our will for His.

In the following example we are going to see a greater work than the plucking of a coin from the mouth of a fish. We shall see a living death defeated, a lost soul recovered, a warped and twisted mind restored, a tormented person made whole and happy and useful.

Ten years ago, while the Pastor was preaching his Sunday morning sermon, a woman rose in the congregation and leisurely walked to the front of the sanctuary. The offering had been received and the plates were on a table. As casually as any act could be she began to pick up the envelopes and money. Like a miser gloating over coins she let them drop through her open fingers to fall upon the table and floor. Some of the money she stuffed into her overcoat pockets. The congregation sat fixed, startled, horrified.

One of the men of the choir left his place and started toward the woman. Instantly she grabbed the offering plates and hurled them at him, scattering the remainder of their contents all over that part of the church. As she threw the plates she also let loose a verbal barrage, "Your silver and gold!" she yelled, her face contorted, her eyes flashing fire. Her tones were charged with hysterical venom and contempt.

Before the man could reach her she had thrown a basket of flowers at the choir, shouting, "The idea of you women being in here without your hats on!" Flowers and water went everywhere. By now another man had reached the immediate scene and the woman was soon overpowered. She wrestled and screamed and kicked and yanked as the men hurried her down the aisle toward the door. As she was being pulled through the door she cried in a loud voice, "What a shame!"

Said Pastor Brown: "I had stopped preaching when the woman began to appropriate the money. I stood there wondering what would happen next. At the moment I seemed unable to gather my thoughts and actions into any kind of effectual pattern. I was grateful to our choir member for his ability and presence of mind."

No doubt many of you who read this will recall a similar situation in your own experience where you too were rendered helpless momentarily. When you did finally act it was probably upon an urge or compulsion from within. You acted upon a subjective guidance rather than upon any power of objective reasoning. When action came to Pastor Brown in this instance it was motivated by a flash from within and not by any deliberately thought out course of procedure. What actually occurred in his mind was the work of the Holy Spirit. The highest form of guidance in which the Holy Spirit is involved is the guidance that comes through His own Word, the Word of Scripture. "He will bring all things to your remembrance," said Jesus, "and will guide you into all truth." He does this, not apart from His Word, but by means of His Word. Hence may we note carefully how this is done in this particular emergency, for there was brought to the Pastor's remembrance the passage of scripture that caused the minister to do the right thing at the right time in the right way. Said Pastor Brown:

"When the door closed behind the woman I suddenly recalled a similar incident recorded in the fourth chapter of Luke's Gospel, where a man with an unclean spirit rose in a service while Jesus was preaching. This man, like our woman, interrupted the meeting, and broke in upon the message. But in that case the officials did not come forward to drag the man out by force. Instead Jesus digressed from his sermon to the many and fixed his attention upon the needs of the one. Instead of casting the sick man out of the church he cast the evil spirit out of the man, and healed him then and there. All this went through my mind in a flash of time, while the congregation sat petrified, for they did not know what the demented woman would do next."

May I urge you to pause and ponder this information. And let me repeat that there is no higher guidance than that of the Holy Spirit using the Word of God to instruct men, especially in emergencies like this, and also during times when we are counselling with a person about his problems or difficulties. If the counsellor is passive and thus receptive the answer and solution will come through to the person, and it will be in the form of an apt scripture, fitting the situation exactly and filling the need perfectly. Everything synchronizes when the Holy Spirit is in charge.

In this case you will observe that Pastor Brown had first been rendered ineffectual, inadequate to do anything objectively. He was unable to think with his outer, reasoning mind. His mind had been disconnected, and while his body was tense his mind was passive.

"In the front pews," the Pastor continued, "were some twenty-five persons who were visiting our church for the first time. They were members of the Immanuel Baptist Church made famous by Dr. Johnston Myers. The church had sold its building, and some of its members were shopping around in search of a new church home. So they had come to our church that Sunday morning to see about placing their membership with us. Thus they were occupying the front pews. Literally they had a ringside seat at this exhibition of madness, and it was a question as to whether they were in a church or a lunatic asylum. Had I been greedy for members this incident would have dealt me a painful blow.

"Remembering what Jesus had done," Pastor Brown went on, "I suddenly came to myself. I was calm and self-possessed. My whole being seemed to have been lifted to a high, fine level of consciousness. I explained to the congregation that the woman was sick; that she was not to blame for something beyond her control. I said that instead of fearing and condemning her we must have faith in God for her and love her, even as Jesus loved her; that we must pray for her and all together commit her completely and utterly into the merciful hands of the Father.

"We got still and prayed for the woman, who was now raving and struggling on the street in front of the church. As we prayed the madness and tension went out of her as a current goes out of a wire when the circuit is cut. She grew quiet and came once more into her right mind. With a sense of shame she began to apologize for her conduct, and to return the money she had taken. But she had not been completely healed by our prayer. In a few days she was committed to the state hospital at Elgin, Illinois. Some weeks later I went out to see her. She received me as a thirsty man welcomes the sight of fresh water. She seemed so forlorn and pathetic, and she wanted to pour out her heart and soul to me in confession."

You will notice in what follows a fine example of expressive psychotherapy and will realize the value of confession. This is a highly efficacious way of treating hysterical disease; but the one receiving the confession should be free of judgment, loving of heart, and powerful in faith. The Pastor continued:

"I had a feeling that the woman's condition was mainly due to an accumulation of mental and emotional rubbish, a guilt-consciousness organized around some past mistake. So I allowed her to pour it all out on my listening ear. She told me of hidden, secret things that would drive anyone insane. But when she had unburdened herself she felt better, as though a heavy load had finally been lifted from her heart. We then knelt together in prayer. I invoked the all-compassionate Jesus, asking him to forgive every mistake in the life of this suffering child, to cleanse her mind of guilt and her heart of shame. I invoked the Holy Spirit and asked Him to make her receptive to His redeeming power, to restore her heart and mind, to release her arrested soul, to fill her with His wondrous joy and Love and Grace."

The Pastor looked up. His eyes were misty. His voice was tender with thanksgiving when he concluded.

"From that hour," he said, "her recovery was certain. She was promptly transferred to a cottage. A few weeks later she was discharged as cured."

A shattered mind, a shame-scarred heart, a confused will, an earth-bound soul, a pain-torn body! And then the mind returned, a heart made clean and peaceful, a will restored and committed, a dull soul loosed. "The works that I do shall ye do also, and greater works shall ye do, because I go to the Father."

Perhaps there should be some further word on the ministry of the Holy Spirit. The Third Person of the Trinity has been too much neglected by educated ministers. His work seems especially efficacious in mental cases. In the following chapter, among other things, I shall use one illustration, a case of insanity, which will show how quickly the Spirit works when the conditions have been established for His intercession. His guidance is instant when the heart is ready.

Chapter VII . . . . .

When Holy Spirit Commands

"Evil Goes"

MAY we now briefly review the previous chapter. We saw Pastor Brown come under the guidance and power of the Holy Spirit. The result was a correct handling of a ticklish situation. This power, manifesting as Love for the disturbing woman, who in this instance was an enemy, resulted in the glorification of God through the victim's recovery. The guidance of the Holy Spirit manifested itself in what he said and did during the emergency.

The Spirit impels and compels.

Let us examine these evidences. In the beginning Pastor Brown was compelled. His objective mind was momentarily short-circuited, and he stood there helpless and ineffectual. Now he did not short-circuit his objective mind. It was done in spite of him through the situation that arose. With the objective mind disconnected for an instant his subjective mind was exposed and the Holy Spirit invaded it with power, direction, and information. It was then that he *came to himself,* i.e., when he came back into his objective consciousness. But now that mind was a different mind. Whereas it had been the master of the subjective mind it was now the willing servant, and acted as a servant ought to act. In all this the Pastor was compelled.

May this point be emphasized. Unless the objective,

everyday mind is surrendered, along with the personal will, the Holy Spirit can have no access to the personality. He must wait upon this abdication, and in well-timed emergencies, as we have seen, He can of His own accord bring it to pass. The objective mind is identified with the factual world: the subjective mind with the spiritual world. The Spirit instructs man's subjective consciousness as in sleep for instance, and these instructions are utilized in the world by the willing cooperation of the objective consciousness, and become the works of the Spirit. The works done by man have no spiritual value; but the works done by the Spirit through man are always edifying and redemptive. The objective mind, undisturbed by the Spirit, deals only with man's business. The objective mind used by the Spirit is always about the Father's business. "Wist ye not," says the Christ within, "that I should be about my Father's business."

Let us now observe the second point. After Pastor Brown's objective mind had been cut off momentarily under compulsion, arbitrarily compelled by the Spirit, he was then persuasively impelled. He did not have to carry through according to the Spirit's design, but he was inspired to want to do so, and did. When again he spoke it was under the guidance of the Spirit's desire. Also, he followed clear through on the case by his own free-will and volition. Thus he removed his initial Love and faith from the abstract and put them into the concrete, out of the theoretical and into the practical. This is what is meant by the Word made Flesh. Finally at considerable sacrifice and personal inconvenience he went all the way out to Elgin, Illinois, to call upon the patient.

The Third Person of the Trinity has been woefully ignored, both by the regular churches and by the irregular nonchurched groups all over the world. As a student of religion your attitude toward the Holy Spirit has probably been unfavorably colored by what you have seen in the emotional holiness cults. You may have said many times: "If Holy Spirit religion causes people to perform as I have seen and heard them, I want nothing to do with it. They have acted more like unbalanced minds than like sane persons."

That commentary may be answered after this manner: Every virtue is capable of being abused. There will always be queer people to *queer* sound doctrine. The doctrine, however, will remain sound no matter how unsound it is made to appear by unsound persons. The principles of electricity are sound and eternal. Nor would anybody ignore and reject them and their benefits simply because many queer people inspired by greed misuse these principles in cut-throat competition and destruction.

The ministry of the Holy Spirit is the greatest ministry in the world. It is the supreme power in the world, and we should not abandon the Spirit because others make Him seem more like a cosmic lunatic than a Benevolent Deity. We may here describe the Holy Spirit as the Whole Spirit. If this be a true estimate of Him, then those who come under His influence will act as whole persons.

There is an intimation to the contrary in the New Testament. Those who were baptized by the Holy Spirit at Pentecost were held up as abnormal in their conduct and behavior following their experience, "as drunken on new wine." The truth about it is seldom mentioned. In reality they acted as whole persons ought to act. But this was in such violent contrast to the contemporary, limited life of that day that it seemed to be unusual, even abnormal. All the student needs to remember is, that this accusation of drunkenness really came from enemies of the Spirit and not from the Spirit Himself. Peter voiced the Spirit's word, and it was a prompt denial. "For these *are not* drunken, as ye suppose." In fact, they had suddenly become normal and whole, and this state of the abnormal and partial seemed "off," just as a rational man seems irrational to a crazy person.

It is very easy to be self-deceived about the Holy Spirit. It is quite simple to whip up the emotions and call the state a Holy Spirit experience. Under this deception people can and do have a wonderful time, give vent to their wild, frustrated emotions and unfulfilled desires under the guise of Holy Spirit religion without being accused of borderline insanity. But there is no sacrifice or personal discomfort involved, and sacrifice is likely to be the acid test of the authenticity of the experience.

A group of people may band together. They may engage in a furious exhibition of emotional abnormality. They may give vent to their wild, frustrated emotions, and shout and scream and yell until they are blue in the face, even as did the demented woman. In this way they are artificially set free from the ordinary restraints imposed by conscience and conventional demands. They may in this way use the Holy Spirit as an excuse for license and personal indulgence. They do have a good time in the absence of sacrifice and discomfort. It is but another way to induce an escape mentality, and side-step for the moment the hard, bleak, and painful actualities of life. Under the delusion of "being filled with the Holy Spirit" they may resort to licenses which normally would convict them of insanity or eroticism. And this good time they have together may not be far removed from the good time achieved by a group of alcoholics who gather in a tavern instead of a church.

You are probably aware that the fellows of the tavern are not inclined to end their binge in an act of charity and self-sacrifice. Neither is this likely for those who imagine they have become drunk on the "new wine."

Observation is almost certain to prove this one thing: persons who are deluded into believing they are agents of the Holy Spirit will talk much and do little. They are like writers and artists who talk shop incessantly but never get around to writing or painting. We should consider as suspicious, therefore, those who talk endlessly about the Holy Spirit, but who have no works of Love and faith to back up their claims.

One more point about the action of the Holy Spirit. If there is any unloving judgment, condemnation, criticism, or negative reaction against other persons, the Holy Spirit claim is spurious, for His directions are always loving and affirmative: never resentful and negative.

In the ministry of Pastor Brown I find these authentic evidences of the Holy Spirit. He does not shout and yell; he does not display an emotional jag. His ministry is quiet, persuasive, and reassuring. His Love follows through into corresponding actions, and his faith is supported by the testimony of redemptive works. He thus has the authority to speak about and under the Spirit. I feel his ministry can meet the Spirit's most rigid test. Too, I am sure you will feel the same way after you have finished "When A Doctor Prays."

I recently reported this healing from the pulpit in New York City. Afterwards a man came up and said: "That is the most faith-inspiring thing I've ever heard. But it seems unbelievable." My reply was: "The proof is on file. You are free to check the case."

Chapter VIII . . . . .

When A Doctor Prays

"Complications Are Overcome"

SUPPOSE there was someone you loved more dearly than your own life, and that one had passed into the final coma with only a little time left before the quick snapping of the frail cord which has held your loved one to this world. How would you feel? Would you join the verdict of medical science and give up? Would you, too, turn away and say, "There is no hope; the one I love must die?"

You are going to see the power of God at work in just a moment. You are going to see a demonstration of faith and Love that will amaze you, stimulate you. You will see fulfilled the mighty truth that "with God all things are possible." Before your eyes you will see an actual realization of the promise of Jesus: "And whatsoever things ye shall ask in my name, that will I do, that the Father may be glorified in the Son. If ye shall ask anything in my name, I will do it."

You have probably been wondering about the healing power as you have seen it expressed through Pastor Brown. Hints have been given as to the secret of that power. Love and faith! But what are these elements? Well, they are the links between men and God. It is by means of Love and faith that man has communion with God.

Now what does communion mean? Let me tell you exactly what it means. Communion means partnership. If you and I were associated in business we should be partners. What is partnership in the world life becomes communion in the spiritual life.

Let your thoughts span the centuries. You pause at a strange scene. A boy of twelve stands in the midst of a group of spiritual leaders. His parents have come in search of him. He says to them, "Wist ye not that I should be about my Father's business?" Yes, God's work in the world is a *business,* and we are His *partners.* In the world He must do His work through the bodies and minds and souls of men. He can work from the spiritual world down into the mortal world only by means of *partnerships.* Pastor Brown is a partner with God in the greatest business enterprise in existence. His Love and his faith have made him a partner in this business, even as Love and faith will make partners of us, if we are willing to yield to the requirements of Love; if we are willing to take Love out of remote theory and put it into practice among our fellowmen.

As you come face to face with the following deathbed scene keep in mind the scripture, "With God all things are possible." Also the scripture, "If ye shall ask anything in my name, I will do it." Just anything. No matter what it is. No matter how seemingly absurd, unreasonable, impossible, to the limited human mind! Look again at that firm, positive, uncompromising promise, "I will do it."

"I will not just think about it, or take it under advisement. If you ask in my name, I will do it."

How prone we are to fail these mighty promises in the flabby weakness of our faith, in the heady wine of our worldly wisdom! And failing, how eager we are to excuse ourselves, to rationalize our miserable doubts, "to sickly o'er with the pale cast" of hypocrisy the cheap and tawdry condition of our confidence in God! That Jesus can stand our clever alibis and educated affectations is surely a demonstration of his Love and superhuman tolerance.

Being caught in the limitations of mortal thought I must admit that I was surprised at the healing that I am about to relate. That prayer could cast out an obsession from the personality of Frank did not tax my belief so much. That cancerous tissue, under the impact of faith, could be changed into healthy flesh was a possibility I could take in my stride; but when a woman could be called back from the last coma, from the very edge of death, I could only wonder and marvel at the awful, unspeakable power and mystery of an answering God.

There was a physician in Pastor Brown's church, splendidly skilled in the dogmas of medical science, who, thank God, was able to bow in child-like trust before a higher power and see what things a loving God can do for those who believe. He was counted among the eminent physicians on Chicago's South Side. On a certain Sunday afternoon he phoned Pastor Brown and asked for an immediate conference. His voice was urgent and heavy with a feeling of distress. It carried to Pastor Brown's ear a pronounced anxiety and deep concern. When he arrived at the parsonage the cause of his emotional disturbance was made known.

He had just come from the hospital where one of his nurses was dying with heart trouble, pneumonia, and septicaemia. Even now she was in the coma, that mysterious realm that lies between this world and the next.

She had been put into an oxygen tent to prolong her flickering life a little while. She was running a high temperature, and she was all but pulseless. The doctor stated frankly that there was nothing further he could do; that his nurse was receiving everything known to medical science; and that unless God did something quickly she must die.

RECOVERY

And so, in his desperation and helplessness, he had come to his pastor. He had come in search of that something greater than all the skills of medical practice. He had come seeking a contact with the "God of all Grace."

The promise of Jesus, "I will do it," hung like a challenge over the little group who had gathered in the Pastor's study. There was the doctor himself, the Pastor, and the Pastor's wife. These three. And all unseen, the God whom they earnestly sought.

If two or three will gather together "in my name," and if they will agree together that "I am able, I will be in the midst of them, and they may ask whatsoever they will, and I will do it."

They all dropped to their knees. The doctor prayed first. He opened the floodgates of his heart to God. He prayed as only a truly great and burdened man can pray, weeping unashamed, even as Jesus wept in his compassion over a dying Jerusalem.

Pastor Brown prayed next. He did not hedge or equivocate. He prayed boldly, fearlessly, faithfully. He did not hesitate on any notes of doubtful speculation. There was no fumbling in a fog of controversy. He did not excuse a lack of faith by tagging on the terminal line, "Thy Will be done." He took it for granted that it was God's Will to heal the nurse. He laid claim to the unmodified promise, "I will do it." It was only then that he committed the dying woman to God's perfect Will.

The Pastor's wife then offered up her intercession on the patient's behalf. She asked for a complete healing, and a demonstration of God's power and glory.

With her "Amen" the three rose, and the doctor went back to the hospital. He was met by the patient's nurse, who said, "I am able to detect her pulse now, and her temperature is slightly lower."

With this the doctor's heart expanded with a new hope. It began to beat out a rhythm of gratitude. He went immediately to his home to wait for the next report. It came an hour later. The patient's temperature was dropping rapidly. Her pulse and respiration were growing stronger by the moment. Something strange and beautiful had happened. Some curiously new and unknown power had entered in, and the patient was responding to Life with life.

On the following day the nurse was normal. Color had returned to her face. She was sitting up in bed, now free from the need of artificial oxygen. She had indeed come back from that unknown gulf that lies fixed between two worlds. Within a few days her strength had returned, and she was discharged to resume her duties.

"If ye shall ask anything in my name, I will do it." Anything! Yes, even the recovery of this woman, though she had gone into that valley of the shadows from which few travelers may ever hope to return.

This physician is now a deacon in Pastor Brown's church. He is also the chairman of the church's finance committee. Frequently he gives talks in the church during prayer meeting. And once each year he preaches a Sunday sermon. On one of these latter occasions he testified to the raising of his nurse, and thus witnessed powerfully for God.

Pastor Brown says that to hear the doctor relate this story is a profound and moving experience, for he is essentially a scientist not given to sudden flares of public piety and emotional outbursts of religious zeal. When he reaches the point in his story where he proclaims the evidence of the hospital chart the hearts of the people are stirred and their spirits are quickened. For that chart reveals that the nurse's recovery began while the three were on their knees in prayer.

Preaching sermons about God's Love and grace and power has its place. Writing books about the healing ministry of Jesus has its place also. But one living testimony and witness to God's Love and grace and power are worth more than a thousand sermons and a hundred books which can only tell about the power and grace of a loving Father. The world may need the sermons and books. But it needs far more. It needs influential men and women who believe in a power greater than the human mind, and who are willing to fall to their knees before God and experience His power in their puny, limited lives.

The world needs education, yes, and educated classes; but one educated man who, out of personal experience, can bear witness to God, is worth more to the world than a million educated men who can only refine human selfishness and dignify doubt with an assumed air of sophistication and professional cynicism.

If the world had more praying doctors, statesmen, educators, scientists, politicians, publishers, businessmen, workers, preachers, movie producers, there would be less exalted ignorance in high places, and less war-breeding and pestilence in low places.

Education in the absence of God's Love is a hundredfold menace to humanity. But education with a witness of God's Love is a thousandfold blessing to humanity.

"It would be good," said Pastor Brown, "if more physicians had the authority to quote, 'I am the Lord that healeth thee.' "

Chapter IX . . . . .

Is Health Of Soul Contagious?

"An Injured Brain Healed"

ETHEL TULLOCH BANKS, writing in the magazine, *Sharing,* for April, 1946, said this of the healing ministry of Jesus:

"When his friends came to share their most treasured memories of Jesus, they shared incidents of his ministry of healing on page after page after page of the Gospels. The most cheering and stimulating and healing reading for the sick are the case records of the Great Physician by Matthew, Mark, Luke, and John. Their wonder and pride and delight burst forth into words—'He laid his hands on every one of them, and healed them. He went about all the cities and villiages . . . healing every sickness and every disease among the people. . . . As many as touched him were made perfectly whole. The multitudes wondered when they saw the dumb speak, and the blind to see.'

"But what news about God do the followers of Jesus take to the sick today? Do they speak joyously of God's Will to heal? Of God's power to heal? Let each answer the question out of his own experience. I fear that very few visitors speak with the glad, confident faith of the earliest followers of Jesus."

And yet there are those few among the Christian ministers of today. When they visit the sick they do not come in clothed in a dark robe of gloom, counselling Christian resignation and a stern endurance of the inevitable. They come with the glad tidings that Jesus still lives and heals, even as in the good old days of infant Christianity. There are a few who can still say, "Here am I, send me, Lord." They walk and talk in an atmosphere and tone of confidence and faith in the power of God to cure.

Among these few we are using Pastor Brown in this book as a typical example. His bedside manner is not doubt but trust; it is not imitation but emulation; it is not a professional sympathy, but a genuine out-flowing compassion for the one who suffers. He approaches the sick with a firm, cheerful conviction that it is God's Will to heal. And somehow his contagious faith and optimism is transmitted to the patient, stimulating faith and confidence in him also, inspiring him to a high degree of expectancy, so that when they pray the patient is in the mood to receive and accept the health and Love of God.

The case of Miss Frances Reid is an excellent example of how faith can be transferred from a person who has it to one who lacks it. The principle is that good is even more contagious than evil, health than sickness; that love excites love and faith excites faith. If a man has the disease of doubt he can transmit it to another. If he has confidence he can transmit that. If he has the Spirit of God he can pass it on to others. What he has he can share. If he believes in God's willingness to heal he can loose this belief in the sick. The good is always transmissible.

Miss Reid was badly injured in an automobile accident. Upon examination in St. Luke's Hospital, Chicago, severe internal injuries were discovered. But these were minor compared to a brain injury, which was diagnosed as concussion.

IS HEALTH OF SOUL CONTAGIOUS?

When Pastor Brown heard of the accident his heart went out to Frances. He went immediately to her bedside, where he found her in the throes of agonizing pain. He suggested a period of clinical prayer, and not a period of formal, half-doubting prayer as a dubious means of awakening in her a resigned sense of enduring what could not be cured. His air and attitude were hope-inspiring. In spite of her pain his optimistic faith got through to her consciousness, and she quickly and eagerly accepted his offer of prayer.

Miss Reid herself, after the prayer, described her experience: "While you were praying, Pastor, I felt as though I were being lifted from my bed. Though I can't find the words, it seemed as though I were actually being held in God's hands. It was such a precious feeling of security. Who could ever tell it? Language fails me. And the feeling is still so vivid to me."

"If I be lifted up I will draw all men to me." In prayer the Pastor had lifted up Jesus as a living, vital, redeeming, healing Presence before the injured woman, and in a strange, beautiful and superphysical way Jesus in turn had lifted her up. For this there is no vocal explanation. Nor is one needed. The important thing is the result, the fruit of faith and Love. This result we have in the Pastor's own words:

"The pain instantly and completely disappeared. It seemed to Frances as though nothing was wrong. She was soon discharged from the hospital fully cured."

Chapter X . . . . . .

Absent Treatment

"Headache Banished"

DURING the whole of his eighth grade year, and all through his high school years, Clair Bass had suffered with violent headaches. At least one day a week he was out of school and in bed.

Several doctors had tried to help him but had failed. Finally he went to an oculist. This man told him that the trouble was the result of muscular strain behind the eyeballs. An operation was advised and the date for it was set. As the time drew near the boy became anxious to the point of dread.

Pastor Brown took the initiative. "Clair, would you want me to pray about this? I'd be happy to do it if you wish." The boy's response was immediate. "Yes, I would, Pastor," he said.

They went into the Pastor's study, relaxed their minds and bodies, and began to seek union with God. Pastor Brown opened the New Testament and read slowly from the story where Jesus touched the blind man's eyes and healed them. They began to meditate upon this healing. As they continued in prayer and found themselves growing in complete and perfect accord they felt the nearness of the Divine Presence. This feeling grew upon them, and they both felt that Jesus could do for Clair what he had done for the blind man.

The Pastor then stood behind the boy and prayed. He placed his hands on Clair's head, letting his fingers rest lightly over the eyes. They were in the study for forty-five minutes, and when they separated both felt that the prayer had been answered.

It was several months later before Clair gave his testimony in the church. He stated that from the time they prayed he had not experienced another headache.

The boy's second healing through prayer came some time after his testimony. He had fallen victim to a bad stomach disorder, which was so pronounced that he had been put on a special diet. Here again Love and faith brought the healing.

In the third healing there was evidence that in the realm of Love and faith the factors of Time and Space do not operate as obstacles. The observing reader, however, will note the element of therapeutic suggestion in this example as it was in the eye example.

This time there was something of the dramatic and spectacular involved. But apart from the methods employed the healing in itself was arresting.

Now Clair Bass was in the South Pacific Theatre of war. For six months he had been suffering with heat rash, in pain most of the time. In addition a fungus growth had appeared above his instep. For weeks he had worn a shoe from which the leather had been cut so as to fit around the infected part.

"Clair and I corresponded frequently," said Pastor Brown. "In one of my letters I suggested an experiment in absent treatment. I quoted appropriate scripture for such an experiment to show him that in God there was no limitation of time or space; that with God all things were possible to those who could believe; but that, nevertheless, it would not hurt the effort if we took time into account. I didn't know where Clair's ship was located, that being a military secret, so that place could not be considered. I suggested that he set a day and hour for our togetherness in prayer, far enough in advance so that we could both arrange our time for the spiritual tryst, he on board his ship and I in my home here in Chicago."

Clair Bass proceeded to work out the schedule, a rather complicated timetable, with the help of the ship's officers. The ship was beyond the international date line. In Chicago the hour set for the prayer period was 11:00 A.M., September 25th. With Clair it was 1:00 A.M., September 26th.

The lad had been instructed to lie down during the experiment and to commit himself to God's Love, trying all the while to let the Presence of Jesus come to him, and to imagine that his pastor was right there beside him in prayer.

"I will be there in spirit," Pastor Brown wrote, "because when two are united in God, they are together in one place, in one accord. With real Love it is always *now* and always *here.*"

The result of this experiment was of course revealed to Pastor Brown by mail. And fifteen months later the Pastor heard the report from Clair's own lips. The boy was now in the full flush of health. He told how he had kept the tryst, and how he came into a consciousness of God's vivid Presence. He said that within a few days the heat rash was gone, never to return, and that the fungus growth on his foot was completely healed. At the time of his experiment his ship was standing off the Island of Mindanao in the Philippines, a distance of ten thousand miles from Chicago.

What shall we say about the mystery of Love and faith which conquers Space and hurdles the barrier of Time? I suppose the best thing to say is, "Attain that kind of faith and Love and see for yourself."

In his last written message to the world, penned shortly

before his martyrdom, it was fitting that St. Paul should speak of holy affection as being the Master Key to life which opens the door to the Holy Spirit. He had been sounding this note all through his turbulent ministry. Now in his old age mellowed to his inmost depths by the kind of Love he had long sensed and preached, he addressed his final word to the churches of Asia Minor. Perhaps our Bible copy is the only copy of that remarkable letter to remain. We know it as *Ephesians.*

In chapter three, verse 18, we find these words: "May be able to comprehend with all saints what is the breadth, and length, and depth, and height." The following verse gives the Key to this kind of extra-dimensional comprehension: "And to know the Love of Christ, which passeth knowledge, that ye might be filled with the fullness of God." For with this Love in our hearts we have the faith required for the next affirmation: "Now unto him that is able to do exceeding abundantly above all that we ask or think, according to the power that worketh in us." Against this Love there is no Time and no Space.

Chapter XI . . . . .

Spiritual Electricity At Work

"After Surgery, What?"

FOLLOWING her abdominal operation complications had appeared and Mrs. Opal Hamilton was sinking rapidly. Looking at the sick woman Pastor Brown did not foolishly deny her condition, thereby insulting her intelligence and committing an outrage against facts. But let the Pastor report the case:

"Opal's surgeon telephoned me of the patient's critical condition," he said. "Unless a change came soon for the better he felt that she would die.

"This was the actual state of affairs. In the earth realm her sickness was a hard, cold fact. On the other hand, in heaven, where the Father lived, there were no such facts. If the patient could be borne up to the Father on the wings of clinical prayer and redemptive Love, the Father could in turn bestow upon her the blessing of His favor, according to His Will and Wisdom.

"Laying my hands upon her it was as though an electrical circuit had been closed."

This parabolic language may seem a little strange. But there is something in the touch that is in the nature of a connection made in a broken power line. We remember the healing that took place at the Gate Beautiful when Peter, filled with the Love power of Pentecost, took the hand of the beggar who had been crippled from birth, and healed him. When Peter touched the man he was connecting the need with the supply. God was the supply; the cripple was the need; Peter was the connecting link between the two. The healing current was nothing less than Love, a saturation of which Peter had just received in the experience of the Upper Room.

At a certain training school for Christian workers I observed two water fountains, one to the left of a hall and one to the right. I noticed the students invariably went to the fountain on the right. I enquired into the reason for this seeming preference. The girl laughed and replied, "The other fountain is not connected with the water supply." The thirsty students were drawn to the fountain that could fill their needs.

Recently I was on my way East from the West Coast. The beautiful streamlined coaches were receiving passengers; but for some reason the powerful engine had been removed temporarily. Those coaches represented the best in passenger train equipment. But good as they were they could not move, they could reach no destination until the engine, the train's power supply, had been connected once more. The coaches were the need, the engine was the supply. Put the two together and the train would move.

In this case Pastor Brown put himself in union with the power of God. Then by touching the sick woman he connected her with the Source of supply which had correspondence with her need. When he made the connection by touch he felt God's healing energy pass through him to the suffering patient. How many ministers enter their pulpits with an eloquent sermon who have not previously taken time for prayer, for getting into union with God's power! The sermon is beautiful. It is pulpit equipment of the highest order, like the streamlined coaches. But without being connected with the Engine of God, will it move the congregation toward its spiritual destination?

RECOVERY

Some time ago I was a guest speaker at a Sunday morning church service. As we waited behind the scene for the moment of entry the minister was nervous and paced back and forth. With only another minute to go he said, "Let us pray." Quickly he rattled off a verbal petition, seemingly eager to be rid of the drab habit and dull chore. Fortunately I was better prepared, having begun at four that morning to establish union. I had no sermon in mind, not even a text until he called for one, and then I permitted him to make the choice. My need was for power. Given this the transmitting equipment would take care of itself.

First of all Pastor Brown had to connect himself with the power of God. When the connection had been made he laid his hand on the dying woman and prayed in deep faith for her recovery. Said he: "The hospital chart will show the immediate change in her condition. Improvement started as I prayed, and she made a normal and complete recovery."

The abruptness of the Pastor's statement is rather disquieting and may tax the reader's credulity. Then again the constant reference to God may seem vague and remote to some. Can this Power he calls God perform such seeming miracles? And in this matter of healing is it reasonable to believe that some unknown force can be activated and made to work as by magic?

So far you may still be unconvinced in the face of a mounting file of evidences, and your trust may still be fixed in the medical doctors as the sole custodians of healing ability. But do medical doctors really heal? They themselves will be the last to make such claims. As the late Dr. Walter Cannon put it, "Any physician knows that if given rest, proper food and ease of mind 90 percent or more of his patients get well." Does the physician make them well? or does he merely try to cooperate with a Healing Intelligence already within the patient?

If the surgeon removes a diseased kidney the other kidney develops and doubles its size, thus being able to perform the duties of two kidneys. Does the doctor cause this well kidney to start growing? If not, then Who does cause it? In certain kinds of heart trouble that organ increases its size and strength. It may become three or four times larger than normal. What Power brings this about? Is it the power of a doctor?

If that dread disease, peritonitis, has taken over, how can we check its spread? Many times when it has spread too far, you have seen it kill, and render doctors helpless. But don't be hopeless, for there is a foundation for hope in the chapter to follow.

Chapter XII . . . . .

The Power Of Corporate Prayer

"Peritonitis Leaves"

"HE WAS a stranger in our group," said Pastor Brown. "We all liked his personality. Late the next evening I received word that he was critically ill at the Woodlawn Hospital. I went there immediately to pray for him."

As a matter of fact, the man was desperately ill by the time the Pastor arrived, and the nurses in charge felt that he could not survive the night. He had become sick that Sunday morning in Pastor Brown's Bible Class. He had been twenty-four hours in bed without medical attention. When at last he was examined a ruptured appendix was discovered. And though he had been rushed to the hospital, peritonitis, that scourge of surgery, had already begun to permeate his system with its deadly poison.

The next day the Pastor called again, but found no change. He went the following day, and every day for an entire week. Each time he prayed earnestly for the man's recovery; but no sign came to reward his effort even with so much as a ray of hope. Each time when the nurses talked with him about the patient they were grave and said they had never seen any one more sick and still live. Before the week was over the Pastor began to wonder why the man did not improve, or why he did not die, for he was on the edge of death at all hours, day and night. Said Pastor Brown:

"It seemed to me that, although my prayers were not effective as a healing agent, yet they may have been effective in keeping the patient alive, so that God may have been using me nevertheless for some reason known only to Himself."

When the next Sunday morning came the Pastor stood before his Bible Class once more. He told his students about the man, and reminded them how he had been stricken in class on the previous Sunday. He frankly stated that in his opinion his prayer had lacked power, and that he wanted the class to do something a little unusual. He asked them to join their faith with his faith. Then he described the method they were to use.

"I told them," said Pastor Brown, "that I would pray, and that I wanted them to forget themselves; to forget their ordinary ways of praying; to just unite with me spiritually, and to be in such perfect agreement that my words would be their words."

They were to relax themselves, sit passive, receptive, comfortable, while he asked God to do something. "We are not going to do it ourselves," he said. "But let the words of my prayer be the unanimous yearning in every heart here this morning."

He then proceeded to detach himself from his surroundings, while he lifted the young man up to God in the arms of Love and faith. He prayed vocally for God's healing, redemptive power to touch the body and soul of the patient and restore him to health. When he had finished praying he sensed a perfect union in the group, a beautiful oneness of spirit, and it seemed to him that the prayer had been effective. Said he:

"Later that day I heard of improvement in the man's condition. The improvement had begun while we were in prayer. Within two weeks the patient was discharged fully recovered."

It would seem that, whether consciously or intuitively, the Pastor had hit upon a technique here, if it could be called such, for establishing the best possible condition for corporate prayer, for clinical or laboratory intercession, which might be helpful to others who wish to do a work of this kind.

Let us note this particular point: he told the group to *join* their faith to his faith, and not just to *exercise* their faith in his faith. Seemingly his own faith had not been adequate to furnish an avenue for the power of the Spirit. What was needed in this case, apparently, was a pool of faith, a volume greater than he could supply alone. So that each one in the group who contributed a mite of faith added to the common fund by that much.

Another important feature in the method was the unity of minds and hearts in one purpose and in one desire. They were to be receptive and in one accord, loving one another as only a group of spiritual mutuals can Love. Why this is necessary we do not know; but we do have an authoritative example for it.

For if we examine the Pentecost experience in this light we may actually get a revelation of how, for the first time, the Universal Spirit, the *Pneuma* of the pre-Christian Greeks, and the *Breath* of the early Hebrews, was personalized and brought through as the Holy Spirit to those who waited in the Upper Room.

They were in one place. They were sitting around, apparently relaxed, receptive, expectant, loving one another, and creating a volume of faith composed of the fragments of faith contributed by the hundred and twenty who were present. Now this volume of faith in one or even in a hundred may not have been sufficient to channel the personalized Spirit through to the world. But the faith of one hundred and twenty was adequate to bring the Holy Spirit out of the abstract, diffused, universal state into the personalized form, so that the Spirit is no longer "It," an impersonal power, but is now "He," a personal God. He is no longer a "coming" Spirit, but an "arrived" Spirit. He is no longer to be pursued and sought by faith; but He is to be recognized and accepted by faith. He is not coming. He has already come, brought through at the time of Pentecost by the Love and union and the pool of faith to which each of the hundred and twenty made a contribution.

Was not this clinical prayer group, then, a little Pentecost condition? Here each member added his or her bit to the common fund of faith. They were in union one with another, loving one another just as it was at Pentecost.

At any rate, Pastor Brown had believed his own faith to be inadequate in this case. His prayers had failed. But when his faith had been multiplied by the faith of as many persons as were in his Bible Class that morning, a change for the better occurred in the patient, the dread infection was checked, and recovery followed.

We may question the analysis, the explanation; but not the results. The man was dying with peritonitis poisoning, and he recovered. That beautiful fact has glorified the Most High.

Chapter XIII . . . . .

The Most Embarrassing Disease

"Epilepsy Cured"

EPILEPSY is one of the oldest diseases known to man. As it was a mystery to the ancients it remains a mystery to the moderns. There is practically nothing on record pertaining to the cause of this affliction. It seems to be a psychic malady, outside the range of orthodox medical and mental science.

Under its spell the personality is radically changed. The self-consciousness is withdrawn from the objective world and becomes lost to all external correspondences. That it enters an inner world of some kind is certain. But of this interior experience little is known. Medical and mental doctors cannot invade the inner consciousness of another person. They cannot look into this inward realm and report its secrets to the outer curious world. And those who do enter these submerged levels of consciousness return from the adventure with no usable information as to what they have seen and heard and felt. Once they have come back to the marginal life of every day the memory of their experiences is veiled.

No doubt epilepsy is also one of the most embarrassing of all diseases. It lingers before its victim like a plague. It is a dreadful bondage, paralyzing the free movement of the patient, who must always live in mortal fear and terrifying anticipation of the next attack. Being a mystery disease it attracts little sympathetic understanding. Other people are repulsed by the epileptic. He is politely but as surely shunned as the leper.

For the victim of epilepsy the doctors say there is no medical or psychiatrical cure. This would seem to render their cases hopeless. But the healing arts do not stop on the first and second levels. After the physical and mental levels of healing have been exhausted, there still remains a third level, the spiritual. Hence the epileptic is not hopeless. There is always hope for him. For the proof of this we may let Pastor Brown speak:

"For twenty years the woman, a member of my church, was having many epileptic spells every week, and sometimes several each day. Her husband once told me that during the ten years of their married life there had not been a week in which his wife had not had as many as eight attacks.

"One Sunday she was seized during our service, and had to be carried from the sanctuary. The husband had resigned himself to the hopeless verdict of science. But she kept hearing testimonies at our prayer meetings, reports from our people of how they had been healed through prayer. One day she was encouraged to present her case, even though it was said to be incurable. She came to me privately and timidly asked for prayer. My heart went out to her, for she seemed to have a nucleus of faith in God to set her free. I told her I was glad she had come seeking Divine aid, and that I'd be happy to pray for her. Her face lighted up, her heavy heart grew light under the impact of a new hope. We made a compact right then to meet at a certain hour for prayer in her home.

"Somehow, while I was praying for her, I was not conscious of the apparent fatalism with which epilepsy is surrounded. In fact, I had a deep inner feeling that this hopelessness, so-called, in the eyes of God was a false conclusion; but that because it seemed hopeless in man's eyes, it could work to the greater glory of Him in Whom all things are possible. Hence I was able to pray with a vast, confident faith, which bordered well-nigh on a state of knowing. I seemed under conviction of the power of God to heal and release this tormented child.

"I prayed without hesitancy, asking for her complete recovery; that God would eliminate her attacks; that Jesus would command them even as he had commanded the unclean spirits.

"Then I left a few suggestions with her. When she felt an attack coming on she was to take a firm grip on Jesus, declare his name promptly and boldly, to lay hold on his promises, and to allow herself to become invaded and filled with his Presence so that he could protect her from the invasion of the on-coming attack. Thus by admitting an invasion of his Good Spirit she would reject an invasion of some bad spirit.

"The woman, being in great need, took hold of the process and put it into practice. At the end of two months there had been no further attacks. That had been the longest free period in twenty years. Whenever she felt the attack coming she immediately called upon Jesus to invade her life instead, and in each case the onslaught had been repulsed. Never before had she known this experience of witnessing the arrest of a spell once it had begun.

"Nine months passed, during which she had had only one attack. I asked her how she accounted for this exception. She admitted that it was due to inertia and carelessness in not taking a quick refuge in Jesus, and not depending on his protection with a firm and ready faith.

"Shortly after this the family moved and I lost contact with them. That was in 1935. In 1940 contact was again resumed and I learned that the woman had been completely healed."

Chapter XIV . . . . .

The Enemy's Wiles

"Insomnia Overcome"

IN THIS year of our Lord, modern life is meeting with tremendous outer resistance and is suffering with equally tremendous inner tension. Relief is being sought in all manner of artificial ways, but to no avail. One of the effects of this inner tension is the inability to sleep. In this chapter we may note how a man of Love and faith meets the problem of insomnia in our speed-mad age. If you are thus afflicted here is a blueprint for recovery.

Irritations are manufactured by the Devil. Old Nick is that composite aggregration of evil forces known in scriptural language as the Enemy. His work on the human plane is degeneration as opposed to the work of Jesus which is regeneration. In the drama of life, the conflict between the ego and the soul, the Enemy supplies the obstacles in the process of redemption, and God supplies the strength to overcome and gain the victory.

Insomnia is not of God. It is a major obstacle invented by the Enemy, and as such should turn the insomniac to God. "Be still and know that I am God." "Let not your heart be troubled." "Come unto me, and I will give you rest." My peace I give unto you; not as the world (The Enemy) giveth, give I unto you."

In these days of increasing pressure it is not so much

an extension of consciousness that we need. Rather it is a soul-centric intention of the consciousness we now have on hand.

One should never make the mistake of underestimating the Enemy's influence. While he cannot create, he can agitate, invent, and imitate. In fact, he has the most clever and convincing ways of making the best intention appear as the worst. By seeming to agree with our noblest intentions he turns them into his own designs.

Take the matter of prayer, for example. The Enemy does not oppose the prayer impulse. He is too wise for that. He simply injects reason, logic, and doubt, thus rendering the prayer of no account. Let us use an illustration.

Here are two persons who have long been friends. Their friendship has been founded on real Love and mutual confidence. They have passed through many ups and downs together, and because of Love and faith their moorings have held fast. But one day there occurs a serious rift. It slips up on them like a thief in the night. Now their wills clash, their tempers flare, and hot, bitter words sear them to the quick. Soon they are alone and in the silence comes remorse. They have been trapped by one of the Devil's oldest devices, irritation. A sense of shame comes to them, and with it they begin to toy with some good intentions. They may decide to repent and apologize—to make up. This sentiment is dangerous to the Enemy.

His first job is to check instantly this thrust toward humility and apology. Nor does it prove very difficult. He moves in with confidence and makes his appeal to vanity. He says: "If you apologize your good intention will be rejected, and you will be hurt and humiliated. Your apology will make a contribution to the other person's weakness. It will be misunderstood and misinterpreted. Don't do it. Wait!"

You wait, but still you feel ashamed and penitent. You feel as though you must do something to mend the tear and soothe the wound of this broken friendship. You may decide that the best way is to pray about it—together. Now the Enemy is really in hot water. This is the one thing above everything else he must stop. For if two persons take their problem to God together, if together they choke back their hurt feelings, their wounded egos and prides, and kneel side by side in genuine repentance, the Enemy is certain to lose his control of the situation. He must at all cost prevent any joint appeal to God's Love and grace, forgiveness and mercy.

We stated that the Devil uses prayer to gain his ends. And this is how he does it. He appeals to fear and vanity.

"Don't ask the friends to join you in prayer about this problem," he whispers. "Instead pray alone for your friend. This will give you a feeling of large-soulness and sanctity—and justification. It will wipe away your remorse and shame and eliminate the sting of conscience."

And so you pray alone for the one you have injured. You are lulled by your generosity of spirit, and are not aware that your prayer is meaningless in the sight of God. "First be reconciled to your brother, and then come and offer thy gift." You are not even aware that your confession of guilt may be a mere pretense and hypocrisy, and that your prayer for the friend may be a burlesque, a sham, a subtle defense of your egotism, a soothing syrup for your false position, a parrot-like mouthing of vague, devotional words.

On top of all this falsehood the Enemy will persuade you that there is no need to kneel when you pray for your friend. "Remember Pentecost," he will say. "They were not kneeling when they received the Holy Spirit. They were all sitting. So just sit back and relax. No need to assume a humble posture. No need even to pray vocally, or move your lips. Just feel a sense of prayer and indulgence toward your friend. Why be uncomfortable when you pray? Do it the easy way."

Yes, the Devil has wisdom and he knows human nature. He knows that people are instinctively lazy. If they can substitute a resemblance of prayer for the real thing they will do it. Of course those who are advanced in the spiritual life can sit in silence. But such ones are not lazy. They are so alert that the Enemy cannot impose upon their passivity. They are attentive to God. If the Enemy can get the novice in prayer to imitate the liberties of the saints then he has the situation under control. He can make the praying amateur believe that posture is of no importance, and thus laziness promotes haziness.

The Enemy is greatly worried by two persons in trouble if they decide to resolve their difficulty in a recourse to joint prayer. His chief concern is not to oppose prayer, but to encourage it on a fruitless basis.

There are any number of ways the Devil can defeat prayer when it is being done alone. He can cause the petitioner to seek some selfish gift, and ignore the Giver. "Try to realize God," he will say. "Seek a sensation of union with Jesus. Yearn for a miracle to happen to you, a light to flash, a vision to come, a voice to speak, a wind to blow. Seek for signs for wonders, for phenomena, even for your lips to be loosed with a jargon of unintelligible language." This will keep the petitioner's will diverted from the Will of God, and thus block a real undistracted union of wills from being accomplished.

Another way the Enemy can sometimes render prayer useless is by the use of devotional props, such as crosses, candles, and pictures of Jesus or saints when they are used in a superficial and mechanical way. Of course, the sincere accomplished petitioner can employ all these symbols if he wishes, and they may aid him toward the devotional mood and receptive attitude. But the beginner or mere dabbler in prayer can be put at the mercy of the Enemy when he leans on the symbols as a means of escape from the discipline of real communion with God. It is easy enough for the Devil to make the picture of Jesus become a substitute for the Living Presence and Power of Jesus. Sacred objects may at such times become instruments of idolatry.

I have been interested in the prayer life of Pastor Brown, and have observed little room for the Enemy. His prayers are usually guided, not by himself, but by the Spirit. I have previously mentioned three elements which make up the main body of his prayer approach. First, somebody's need; second, God's supply; and third, his own Love-filled and faith-charged petition.

I was requested by a minister friend not to put in the following case, for as he put it, it did not seem to show the healing as accomplished by spiritual power. If this be true, it does nevertheless show an originality of approach. It also reveals the boldness and freedom the Pastor has under the guidance of the Spirit. And this was the important thing.

The woman in question was a confirmed insomniac. Her nights were endless and were spent in tossing and turning. Her days were dreary rounds of weight and weariness. At this time a great fear in the nature of a pronounced phobia had claimed her mind. She was worried constantly. She felt that by losing so much sleep she would die. She could not conceive how a person could go on living without the restorative and recreative effects of slumber.

Pastor Brown, warm with compassion, spoke to her out of knowledge and under inspiration. He proceeded to dispel this devilish idea or fixation from her mind. He told her that restoration could come to the body in repose regardless of whether the consciousness had been detached by sleep; that the actual sleep state was not necessary to the renewal of cell life.

The woman was delightfully surprised to hear this. It gave her a quick sense of relief. As a means of attaining the essential repose the Pastor offered the victim the following method.

Before retiring she was to read her Bible. After a prayer time she was to lie down in a comfortable position and continue in prayer for a while. Then she was to turn the point of attention to her body and try to feel it in a relaxed condition.

Pastor Brown demonstrated:

"I had her sit in a chair loosely and allow her feet to rest easily upon the floor, her head against the back of the chair, her arms hanging limp from their sockets, her hands resting in her lap. After she had closed her eyes I asked her to follow my suggestions.

"I sat in a chair nearby and applied to myself all the suggestions I was offering her." In quieting tones the Pastor began to instruct the woman.

"Think of your left foot weighing ten pounds. Then as weighing twenty pounds. Then as weighing forty pounds." He had her repeat this process with the right foot. Then: "Your feet are now so heavy that it is difficult for you to lift them. You will not even try. You are going to let the floor hold your feet."

This relaxing routine was applied to the calves and the thighs. In fact, with all the parts of the body, including the neck and face and the internal organs. Then the mind was detentionized by therapeutic suggestion, the nerves soothed, the emotions calmed, until all worry and anxiety were gone.

"Now," said Pastor Brown, "you will relax in this manner after you've gone to bed. Once you are relaxed, feel yourself in the very Presence of God, the bed holding up your body, and God holding up your soul. He is above you breathe is of spirit; that it is of God. Imagine that you live and move and have your being. Imagine the breath you breathe is of spirit; that it is of God. Imagine that you are taking in a part of God on every inbreath; and on every outbreath think of Jesus, and his out-flowing Love and wisdom.

"Thus your thought will be immersed in God, in Jesus, in Love, in wisdom. If these are for you what enemy can be against you? In fact, with these on your side it will make no difference whether you sleep or not. His power and blessings are unlimited, and being relaxed and committed to Him you will be ready to receive His bounty."

At this point Pastor Brown began to pray for the woman. He asked God to remove her false worries and destructive fears, and to give her hope and faith and Love. He asked God to dissolve her insomnia, and to grant her an abundance of normal, wholesome sleep, a perfect night's rest every night. Also to bless her home and loved ones.

The Pastor concluded: "This was an unusual procedure from a theological point of view, perhaps; but from God's point of view its authority and efficacy would be determined by its fruits."

"What were its fruits?" I asked.

"They were corrective and redemptive. The patient responded to the treatment. She said it had been a long time since she had been so completely rested and free of inner tension. A week later she was still sleeping every night without much difficulty. At the end of the second week her insomnia had vanished and she was cured."

A few weeks later she yielded her heart to Christ in a ready surrender, and thus found peace also for her soul.

Chapter XV . . . . .

Release Through Relinquishment

"Infantile Paralysis Vanishes"

TO HOW many parental hearts has this compound word struck terror! Not so long ago it struck terror to the heart of my wife and to my heart. We were not the parents; but we had come to love as our own this English boy who had been uprooted and far removed by the Battle of Britain. On a sunny day he had been with us in our yard, full of the joy and wonder of childhood. A few months later the word came that he had been stricken. Our love turned to a dull, throbbing pain.

We entered into prayer immediately. Though his was the most deadly type of infantile paralysis we agreed that God was able to heal him. After an hour came peace, and we knew by an inner, intuitive knowing that our little friend, seemingly hopeless at the moment, would come through his ordeal safe and sound. And he did. At this moment his body is perfect and strong.

Children are exceedingly responsive to Redemptive Love and faithful prayer. In the fight being waged against infantile paralysis the parents of those who have been stricken ought always to pray, to rise out of fear into faith, and out of human love into God's Redemptive Love. For by this means they aid the doctors in charge.

One Sunday morning Pastor Brown came upon a

woman in the primary department of his church. She was heavy with pain and fear. She was weeping. When he inquired into the cause of her distress she said. "My boy is in the isolation hospital with infantile paralysis. The doctor speaks as though he may die."

She had arrived at the Sunday School with one of her other children. The Pastor drew her to one side. He called the teacher of the boys' class, and the superintendent of the department. They all stood in an alcove of the church. Turning to the heart-broken mother Pastor Brown said: "If you knew that it were God's Will, would you be willing to let Billy go to heaven? Could you give him up if you knew God wanted him?"

It was a hard, strange question to put to the mother of a paralysis victim. She pondered the query in her heart, the weight of sacrifice, on the one hand, confronted her, and on the other hand, the pull of possession in a mother's love. After a long struggle with her emotions she said: "Yes. If I knew for certain it were God's Will I'd be willing to release my boy."

Pastor Brown then lifted the child up to God in prayer, surrendering him completely to the mercy and wisdom of the Almighty. Three days later the boy was discharged from the hospital with no sign of paralysis left in his body.

When I recounted these cases to a friend, he commented on the first one in this manner: "Surely every parent prays for his child who has been afflicted with infantile paralysis. Why did God answer your prayer and why does He fail to answer the prayers of thousands of parents?" In this case the healing undoubtedly came more quickly because the mother was willing to relinquish her son completely into the loving hands of the Father no matter which way the Father would choose to take him. It was one of those rare and perfect examples of "letting go and letting God."

Chapter XVI . . . . .

The Invasion Of Love

"A Come-Back After Third Stroke"

"ONE evening," said the Pastor, "just before supper, the phone rang and a close friend of mine told me of a Chicago physician, a beloved friend of his who had suffered a stroke of paralysis. He asked if I could go with him to the North Side and pray for the man. While waiting for him to come and drive me to the hospital, I went into the living room and prayed while my wife finished preparing our meal. It was just six o' clock as I prayed. While praying I felt a vast sense of peace. After supper he came and we drove to the North Side. Before going in to see the patient, I was requested to wait, as the attending doctor had arrived, and was with the patient for some time. Incidentally this attending doctor was the same distinguished physician who flew to Florida to attend Mayor Cermak of Chicago when he was shot with the bullet intended for the late President Roosevelt.

"By nine o' clock I was standing at the foot of the man's bed, looking into his taut, expressionless face. His body was inert, like a corpse. His wife said he had been in that same position since nine that morning without having moved so much as a muscle, without the slightest flicker of a facial expression. Then she suddenly remembered that there had been an indication of life, a slight change of expression which had come over the patient's face about six o'clock. I said nothing. But I was stirred inwardly and I gave thanks silently, for I remembered this was the time I first prayed in our living room.

"Now as I stood there that same peace I had felt lingered as though concern was to be foreign to my heart. To this peace there was added a new invasion of Love for the silent, unmoving man. The Love was like an unearthly affection, and the patient was its object. It was not my human love. This I knew very well. It was a LOVE that had to be written in large capitals. I was greatly inspired by it. It could not be described in any save the most mystical terms. It was like a sweet savor, some nameless, infinite tenderness far beyond and above the human sentiments.

"I prayed with my eyes open, silently, all the while hoping that if it were possible the God of all Grace would invade this man's life, and saturate him clear through to his soul; that his body might be healed for a testimony and his soul released for a witness to God's unimaginable power and compassion.

"It was then that something exceedingly beautiful took place, which filled me with joy and gratitude. When you stand praying and looking into the cold, mute face of a man who is seemingly dead, and you see his eyes open and look into your eyes; when you see his hands move, and his legs; when you see the currents of life flowing once more, stirring through a body, then it is that you must experience the sensation of a strange delight. For it was like watching a man who had died returning to his body and to mortal life. I sat beside him, then, and prayed for him vocally, asking God to raise him out of his affliction."

"Was he healed instantaneously?" I asked.

"It has been my policy through the years, after praying for a person," said the Pastor, slowly, "not to pry into or try to analyze the result. This is always a great temptation. Curiosity is a strong instinct in men. But I have made it a part of my healing ministry to look after the intention and allow God to look after the effects. It has seemed to me that inquiries concerning the outcome would be equal to removing the soil to see if the planted seed were growing. Usually people volunteer the information promptly when they have been healed. But sometimes they take it for granted that I know the results. In this case it was quite awhile before I learned of the outcome. Two days following my prayer at the patient's bedside he was sitting up in a wheel chair, better physically than before his stroke."

Often we hear persons ask: "But what about old people who are ill? Should one pray for them to recover also?" I had many times been presented with this question, and had been a little befuddled by it. So I now passed it on to the Pastor.

"Well," he replied, "Mr. Bevers was an old man. He had passed his 80th year. While visiting with his son here in Chicago he fell ill of a bladder infection, which was described as prostatic tumor. He failed to respond to the medical treatment administered in his son's home. He was then sent to the Jackson Park Hospital where he underwent surgery.

"Late one night his family called to inform me that he was dying; that he probably would not live until morning. I reached the hospital at mid-night to find the aged man in great pain and close to death. I laid my hand upon him and prayed in silence, asking only for God's Will to be done. I prayed that if it were in His divine plan to spare the man's life, then to let His healing grace operate now.

"As I left the room I met the old man's nurse. She told me confidentially that it seemed impossible for Mr. Bevers to live for more than a few hours. Save for the intervention of supernatural power he must surely die soon. In my prayer I had appealed to this higher power. And when morning dawned Mr. Bevers was still alive. Not only was he alive, he was much improved. This to the amazement of those who waited upon him and loved him. He made a rapid recovery, and was soon seen on the streets again, exceedingly active for a man of his years. But when an old person is eager and anxious to go, when he feels that his life's work is done, and to remain as a helpless invalid would be merely adding extra burdens upon those he loves, when such a one is placed completely and prayerfully in God's hands for God's own perfect will to be done, he sometimes goes more quickly and always without pain or suffering right into the loving arms of his Father in heaven."

Chapter XVII . . . .

The Discipline Of Prayer

"Spastic Paralysis Healed"

IF WE assume that every minister is an agent of God for teaching, preaching, and healing, in other words, if he is fulfilling the commission that Jesus gave to his disciples and is trying not to fail on any one of the three levels, and if finally he is successful in all three departments of the Gospel, then it is high time that we may look for the inner secret and the essential reason for his success.

Let us look at the first level, that of teaching. In order to teach the Gospel one must be equipped with organization, concentration, and expression. This equipment can be acquired by study, practice, persistence—by the industry and disciplines which are demanded in the academic processes. To attain teaching equipment or preaching equipment requires application and self-effort. It is acquired by *trying* and perfected by training. But to attain spiritual power, and to contact the redemptive influence which uses the equipment, none of the academic methods are needed. Here self-effort is abandoned. Spiritual power is not acquired by trying. It is bestowed as a free gift of Grace, and is received at the point where one can cease to try; i.e. at the point where one can let go in faith and depend solely upon God.

A man without academic equipment may attain spiritual power; but his reach and range of influence will be drastically limited by the compression placed upon his field of contact and expression. On the other hand, a man may be well equipped and have a wide range of contact; but if he has not been empowered from above he can have little more than a cultural and ethical influence. Both equipment and power are needed by an agent of God.

On the level of healing we find the same thing holds true. One can equip oneself to heal by faith, even as a medical doctor or a doctor of psychiatry becomes equipped through the disciplines of study. But neither the medical doctor nor the psychiatrist does the healing. They and their skills are used by the healing power, which is bestowed to them by Grace.

As one who exercises the healing gift Pastor Brown is well equipped academically. This makes his bedside manner adequate and sufficiently elastic to meet any situation. But this manner is not the healing power. The healing power is Love, and this power is bestowed by Grace, and is sustained by humility, faith, and a disciplined life.

His humility prevents him from taking any personal credit. The healing power comes from God. "Behold, I am the Lord, the God of all flesh: is there anything too hard for me?" (Jer. 32: 27) That is the abiding attitude. Faith in this God of all flesh Who can do the seemingly impossible is the secret of success. The attitude and secret are maintained by the discipline of prayer.

Is it this lack of discipline which causes so many ministers to avoid the healing level of the Gospel? I put this question to Pastor Brown. Said he:

"Sporadic praying needs no discipline behind it. Anybody can pray the occasional and powerless prayer. But to maintain redemptive and corrective power one ought always to pray, even as did Jesus. 'Watch and pray' lest one enter into the temptation of ignoring or slighting God. The healing power is sustained, not by one who prays as fancy dictates, but by one who has made prayer a central habit of life. A praying life is a disciplined life, and the gift of healing, if exercised, is a sacrificial life."

Already we have seen this fact in the healing ministry of the Pastor. He is constantly in the attitude of humility and practice of prayer; and he is ready night and day, regardless of his own comfort, to go in response to any call made upon him for help. He added this further comment:

"For a person to claim spiritual power who does not devote a large portion of his time to prayer is equal to a man claiming fresh air while leaving all the windows down and the doors locked. Fresh air cannot get into a house through blocking walls. Neither can spiritual power get into a man, and flow through him, if all his windows and doors are closed. When a man prays humbly and in faith it is equal to throwing open the windows of the heart and doors of the soul, and letting the clean, vital air of the Spirit rush in."

Now here is a mother who has paid the price for her baby. She has nursed the child and watched it develop. It has now reached the stage where it ought to begin walking. But there has grown upon her a conviction that something is wrong. When the baby attempts to walk one side of its body seems to be strong and the other weak. It keeps falling on one side. The mother's observation grows into an anxiety, and then a fear. She is haunted, as only such a mother can be haunted, with the thought that her child is destined to be a life-long cripple. She fears even to have the baby examined lest her dread be confirmed. Finally she acquires the courage to have this done; the baby is examined, and her worst fears are realized.

Now let us watch her turning to her minister for help, since medical science can offer no hope. Her minister is an excellent teacher of theology and is an inspirational preacher. But he has only an academic equipment. He is equipped to comfort and console this mother, and to help her to adjust herself to the inevitable, to resign herself to the life-long tragedy of her child. But let us suppose that her minister is not only equipped to console the mother but also to be an agent of healing for the child. Let Pastor Brown walk into the situation at this point.

"When the mother phoned me," he said, "I thought of this apt scripture, 'Suffer the little children to come unto me, and forbid them not.' I thought of it because of the identification it had with the problem. The baby's affliction had been diagnosed by one of the leading doctors of the University of Chicago Clinic as spastic paralysis.

"I went to see the child immediately. It was at play in its pen. I noticed that it kept falling. It seemed to have control over one side of its body, and no control over the other side. Its equilibrium had been destroyed.

"As I talked with the mother, comforting her and stirring up her faith, I held the child. I kept my hands upon the affected side. I played with it, gave it attention, and won its confidence and response to my personality. Thus little by little I eliminated the negative reactions an average small child feels in the presence of a stranger. But as I played with the child and talked with the mother I was also responsive to the Spirit Who was making intercession within me. Silently I was asking that Good Spirit to use my hands as I held them on the baby's body. By and by I had the mother enter into a prayful mood while I offered up a vocal prayer. With this I returned the baby to its pen.

"Later the mother informed me that the child was much improved. She had taken the child to the Clinic, and the doctor had reversed his previous diagnosis. What had been described as spastic paralysis was no longer in evidence. He had assured the mother of the child's recovery."

Chapter XVIII . . . .

From Sin To Salvation

"Healing A Soul"

THE prayer of importunity is often difficult. "Knock, and the door shall be opened." It is the prayer commandment of perserverance, of dogged, stubborn persistence in the face of heartbreaking defeat.

One may pray for weeks, months, or even years for the soul of another with seemingly no reward as a fruit for diligence. The human tendency is not to persist against a stone wall of rejection, but to quit and ignore the unresponsive object of prayer.

When a person refuses to respond to our acts of kindness; when we are rebuffed time after time by the one we seek to serve; when there is no apparent yielding or appreciation, we become weary with the thankless effort and turn our attention elsewhere. So it is when we pray for some one in need, when the need does not respond quickly to our prayer. If our prayer continues to go unanswered; if it continues to fall on deaf ears; and if it yields no fruit save the decayed fruit of an endless resistance, we are prone to turn away to one whose heart is less hard and more receptive. No discipline is quite so discouraging as that required by the prayer of importunity.

The attitude of mind that will most surely sustain this type of praying is the one backed up by a certain knowledge and a huge faith. There is a *knowing* in this attitude.

If I know either by external demonstration or by internal experience that prayer is real; that it is dynamic, redemptive, and a corrective, transforming power; that no genuine prayer can return to its sender void, then the object of my prayer and the lack of apparent results lose their importance as a force to defeat me. For I shall realize that the real purpose is the prayer itself; that the act of prayer is its own reward. It needs nothing to justify it but a true motive and an abounding faith. In this way I become less result-minded in my prayer life, so that when I fail to see any results I am not cast down. The one for whom I pray is not my responsibility but my opportunity to seek God and to be found by Him. He is not my problem; but, as E. Stanley Jones has so ably put it, he is God's possibility. He offers me the blessed privilege of responding to God, and that is man's greatest blessing of free will, consent, and choice.

The man was a brother of a Christian physician. He did not know the Lord, and this was a heavy cross for his brother to bear. He was afflicted with coronary thrombosis and diabetes. His brother wanted Pastor Brown to do everything possible that would win him for Christ before he died: for the doctor's own Christian experience had made him doubly sensitive to the brother's real need, that of having his soul released before he crossed over the border into death. The doctor was not uninformed concerning the soul's life beyond the grave. Of course, both the doctor and the Pastor desired a physical healing for the man. But they were more concerned about the healing of his soul. They yearned that he might make the safe passage from sin to salvation.

"I called on the patient at the hospital regularly," said Pastor Brown. "He was always glad to see me and to listen to what I had to say. During these months of his illness we had close fellowship, the doctor and I, praying ceaselessly for his victory. I was always hoping that the Holy Spirit would get through to him, touch his heart, quicken his spirit, and lead him into bondage to Christ and the born again experience. Every time, before leaving, I prayed with him. That he welcomed my visits was revealed in his pithy and sometimes slangy comments when I would eventually show up after an extended absence. Then he would say, 'You're giving me the bum's rush,' which meant I was overwhelming him with my attention. It was his left-handed way of chiding me for my neglect of him. If I saw him near the first of the week he would greet me with a wisecrack, 'How much was the take Sunday?' This was supposed to indicate his conviction that the major business of a church service was to take up a collection. But in his heart there was a genuine respect for the Christian Church.

"He always called me *Rev.* Nor was it uttered in accents of mockery or irreverence. No one else ever used that title, and I knew that in his heart he employed it as a mark of endearment. I loved the man for his evidence of real sentiment. Time after time his brother and I stood or knelt beside his bed and prayed for his body and soul. And we always prayed with compassion and faith. Yet nothing seemed to happen.

"One day the doctor came to my home that we might pray together for his brother who at this moment was dying. Our hearts were filled with Love, and our prayer with emotion. As we prayed the patient rallied, seemingly in response to our earnest intercession. From then on he grew stronger almost daily. He lived an entire year. His brother believes that this respite was allowed by the grace of an answering God—another year of grace in which to prepare his soul for plucking before he wandered into the adventure of death, and into the rich experience of liberation.

"Once while in an oxygen tent he failed to recognize

any one for two days. But when I came in he opened his eyes, lifted himself, and thrusting his hand through the tent, said, 'Hi Rev.' I knew that now between us was the bond that never breaks nor fails.

"More and more his heart melted under Love and prayer. Closer and closer came the Presence of Jesus, tenderly, patiently wooing the man's soul, even as the suitor woos his beloved. At last he could resist the Great Lover of his soul no longer. All barriers went down, and without qualification he gave himself up and accepted Jesus as his Lord and personal Savior.

"He then had a desire to get well so that he might come to the church and give his testimony, to declare his faith in Jesus, and to bear witness to the power of the Holy Spirit, Who leads out of sin and into salvation. Too, he wanted to become an active member of our church.

"Many times I sat on his bed reading and unfolding to him some of the beautiful passages of scripture. So eager was he to attend church, and so improved in body, that on a few occasions it was made possible. His brother and a male nurse would all but carry him in, while others brought pillows and blankets to his pew. He had opened his heart to Jesus and his soul had found redemption.

"One day he fell in his room with a heart attack, from which he did not rally. He went home to God. For his brother the following scripture was fulfilled, 'Thy brother shall rise again.' In this I shared the brother's conviction."

The prayer of importunity! Suppose the Pastor had become discouraged, had given the man up as a fruitless, hopeless case? But he didn't! Thank God!

Sometimes there are oddities in the experience of one who exercises the healing gift. The case to follow will illustrate this. You may doubt that prayer had anything to do with this woman's recovery. The Pastor believes differently. Anyway, the patient was healed, and that is the important thing.

Chapter XIX . . . . .

Inspiration Has Its Inning

"Pneumonia Cured"

PREACHING *declares* what Is. Teaching *seeks* what Is. Healing *claims* what Is. The healing ministry of Pastor Brown is effective to the degree that he can claim the promise of God. In his pulpit he declares Jesus. In his Bible Class he guides those who are seeking Jesus. At the bedside of a suffering person he claims Jesus.

He knows that the healing power is pentecostal. When he puts a hand on a sick person his hope anticipates the Pentecost power for the patient. His faith precipitates that power. And his Love appropriates it. These three, Hope, Faith, Love, and the greatest of these is Love. Given these any minister has the healing gift. For to have these is to have God. And to have these is to do the Will of God.

But how can a man attain them? One of them, Hope, comes into life with us. It springs eternal in the human breast. Men cling to Hope even when nothing is left to cling to Hope. Faith comes into the world with us in embryo, and like any embryo it grows by exercise. When we are born God's Love is potential in us. It becomes an active power when we do His Will. That is why we of ourselves cannot command the emotion of Love, and why we cannot do the Will of God. If we of ourselves try to do His Will we only do our own will. But while we cannot do His Will if we be *willing* He can do His Will in and through us. We cannot Love ourselves divinely; but He can Love us divinely if we be *willing* to let Him. We cannot of ourselves Love a neighbor or an enemy. Our effort to do so would as likely antagonize as to please. But if we be *willing* He can Love the neighbor or the enemy through us. This is the secret of the Christian Way.

What, then, is the most influential department of the threefold ministry? Preaching declares; Teaching seeks; Love claims. Those who Love resemble Christ. The resemblance draws men, as like attracts like. Men will embrace Christ if they see his Love in another, as they will be wooed to the vine which is bearing fruit. A demonstration of Christ is worth more than a declaration or an explanation just as a loaf of bread is worth more than a description of one. Men will believe in God's power to transform character if they see a transformed life. The sick will believe in God's power to heal if they see the glow of health in a Love-filled eye. To be *willing* to Love is to open the door to Love.

In this case we have an illustration. "I will ransom them from the power of the grave; I will redeem them from death."

The woman was suffering from wet pneumonia. The disease had reached the critical stage. One of her lungs had already collapsed. Everything had been done for her that could be done outside the orbit of spiritual treatment. And in so far as Pastor Brown was concerned the application of clinical prayer had also proved ineffective.

During the woman's illness the Pastor had gone to her home several times to pray for her recovery. After she had gone to the hospital he continued in prayer for her. She grew steadily worse. He was praying for her right up to the point of death. At the moment when the doctor and husband knew the end was at hand, Pastor Brown decided to make a final effort. Under inspiration he sent a telegram to his friend, Dr. Glenn Clark, and told him of the seeming hopelessness of the patient's condition. Dr. Clark immediately added his faith to that of the Pastor.

But the woman was on the very fringe of death. What possible miracle could save her now? That miracle entered the case casually the following day. There was nothing spectacular about it. It just strolled in, bowed, and said: "My name is Inspiration. You will act upon me. It will seem like a desperate undertaking to you. But you will do it. For you have no other choice that you can see."

They were inspired to transfer the patient from her home in Chicago to Des Moines, Iowa, where a special treatment could be administered. Though it seemed impossible, the move was made, and the transfer was accomplished without further damage. The treatment was given. The patient began immediately to improve. She soon made a complete recovery. The Pastor remarked:

"Truly God sometimes works in a mysterious way to perform His wonders. From all outward appearance it would seem that this change in medical treatment was the factor in restoring the woman to health. Nor would I imply that it was otherwise. But nevertheless it is interesting to speculate upon a few features of the case. In the first place the decision came to change the treatment immediately after Dr. Clark joined with me in therapeutic prayer.

"Another consideration is the fact that God is not limited to subjective therapy in the treatment of disease. He can use objective means through medical science, for all of the healing arts are but different branches of the main healing Vine. All healing comes from God regardless of the branch which assumes the credit. God has both natural and supernatural means at His disposal. What He creates He can recreate, no matter through whom He works His grace. He is the Author and Finisher of man, and men are only stenographers and assistants to Him.

"When a person asks me, after I have prayed, if he

should cease taking medicine and stop going to a doctor, I tell him to continue, for God may be working through the doctor and his medicine as well as through me and my prayer. Some people have a false idea that the various branches of healing are incompatible one with the other. They imagine that if they are to expose themselves to spiritual therapy they should avoid all natural therapy. Otherwise they feel they are showing a lack of faith. This is a dangerous fallacy and often leads to dire results and fanatical practices, to say nothing of the wilful and deliberate violation at times of state laws. A medical doctor is just as worthy of a patient's faith as is the minister who prays. Both seek the same end by different means, and the recovery comes from the self-same Source.

"I may remind you of an element in this case. Des Moines, where the patient was taken, is the boyhood home of Dr. Clark. It is also the former home of the patient. Neither, however, knew the other. It was a place that both loved, where Divine Love was especially near and dear to them, and Love is the great healing power. While the patient was being treated in Des Moines, Dr. Clark was at the same time conducting a series of Lenten Services there. This may have been coincidence, of course. But it could have been the curious handwriting of God. He does distribute signatures along the roads of life."

Chapter XX . . . . .

Where Two Or Three Agree

"United Prayer Heals Many"

"THEY were all with one accord in one place." (Acts 2:1) They came together with open hearts and humble minds. In this state they were ready to demonstrate Eckhart's truism, "God's divinity comes from my humility." They all knew that it was God's desire to give, and that He could not help giving wherever a heart was prepared to receive His gift.

What if the preparations to receive were perfect enough? Well, in that case, there would be no need to pray for God's grace and fruit. These could then be taken without asking. Prayer humbles the mind and makes the heart receptive. Continuance in prayer keeps the mind humble and the heart open.

In the process of development it is perhaps true that we can have more success in corporate prayer than when we pray alone. The combined faith of several is bound to create a larger body of faith.

"During the Thanksgiving week," Pastor Brown explained, "I announced to my congregation that Mrs. Brown and I were going to have an all night prayer vigil; and that if any of them would care to join us we should be happy to have them come to our home. On the appointed evening seven persons appeared.

"We had thought of spending our time praying for collective interests of the world, for the general welfare rather than for our own personal needs. But when we got quiet and in agreement we seemed guided to leave the general and focus on the personal. So each one was invited to mention any particular need about which we might pray. The first to speak was Mrs. Webster Stark, who was then in the aftermath of poliomyelitis. She was wearing her brace.

"Two years before, while she was bedfast, I had prayed for her and the improvement had been slow and steady. Now she was requesting corporate prayer, not that she might be completely healed, but that through her affliction she might find a closer union with God. She stated that she would rather have the handicap than to lose the spiritual growth and Christian experience that had come to her because of it. Hence we did not ask for a complete recovery, but that her spiritual life might continue to deepen and become richer, leaving the physical healing in God's hands.

"Sometime later Mrs. Stark telephoned to tell me that when the visiting nurse came to give her the next treatment she noticed considerable improvement in her leg, and mentioned the fact. She also wanted me to know that ever since that night of prayer she had been living in a more vital sense of union and joy. Improvement has continued. Now she walks freely and wears no brace.

"Her neighbor, another Parkside woman, was next to request prayer. She told us of her father in Tennessee, who was then quite ill at his home. I enquired into the man's spiritual state, and she said that he was the only member of the family who did not know the Lord. We then prayed that the redeeming grace and Love of Jesus might touch his life and heal him in body, mind, and soul.

"Later she visited her Southern home. She recounted the great change that had occurred in her father's life.

She had mentioned this observation to her mother, who replied that it was difficult to understand, so great had been the shift in her father's behavior. The woman then told her mother about our prayer meeting. When the mother checked back she decided it was about this time that the change of heart began. In addition to this, her father remarked to her one day: 'I'm trying to overcome my temper. But it gets the better of me still, though I'm making every effort.' In all her life our friend had never heard her father speak in this manner. His soul was introduced to a new impulse, which blessed his home, and he recovered from his illness.

"An expectant mother was another who requested prayer that night. She was a deeply spiritual woman who was much loved by all who knew her. In about six weeks a child was to be born to her. We did not know all the facts at this time. She told me later in the hospital, after the baby's birth, that she had wanted to relate to me the wonderful way the Lord had dealt with her the night of our prayer meeting. Up to that time she had been in great discomfort, unable to sleep. But from the night of prayer until the baby was born there had been no distress, and she had slept soundly every night.

"The last person to request prayer in the group was Mable Dukes. For many years she had been suffering with varicose ulcer on her left ankle. This had been an open, running sore for five months. She had been receiving medical treatment in vain. We all prayed for a complete healing. Within a few days the sore started to dry up, and within a week she was able to remove the bandage."

Pastor Brown smiled across the table at our stenographer, and she returned the smile. She was Mable Dukes. She sat there before us a living testimony to the power of God to heal.

Chapter XXI . . . . .

The Connecting Link Of Love

"A Mother And Baby Saved"

"IF THOU canst believe, all things are possible to him that believeth." (Mark 9:23) The longer I sat listening to Pastor Brown reveal case after case of Christian healing the more convinced I became that the teachings of the Gospel were clear and uncomplicated, and that theology and man-invented interpretations were responsible for all the confusions and complexities that had grown up, like weeds, in the garden of Christianity.

I fell to thinking about young people, and wondered why they were so universally bored with church services. It occurred to me that they were bored, not with Christian Reality, but with the dry and fruitless forms into which the Reality had fallen, like a saint among thieves. Why didn't the Christian ministers go to the core of Jesus, and tell people frankly what they would have to do in order to be a believer and a Christian? Why did they persist in their efforts to appease men by whittling God down? Were they fearful of losing their members?

Who is capable of believing that all things are possible? Obviously no unredeemed, once-born person can entertain a belief of this kind. The statement is absurd to the natural man. How, then, can a man become a believer of this sort? Jesus told Nicodemus that we must be "born again"—

"born of the Spirit." If one has been born again one can believe. This is the core of Jesus, his central point of departure. Pastor Brown's faith took its root at this point, when as a boy he was born again. In his church he does not slight or undermine the necessity for being born again. He would hold this up in boldness before his people, and declare the price for it, even if every person in his congregation rebelled at the demand and deserted the fold.

I became persuaded, also, that the successful exercise of the healing gift, like any other great talent, demanded a high degree of concentration, consecration, and self-sacrifice; but that none of these would avail unless they were bestowed to us from Above. Done as a means for self-gain they would leave us alien to God. The processes of the Spirit had support and authority after one had been born again. Prior to that experience they remained imitations, ways to the WAY, but not ways of the WAY.

As no man could succeed in an art or a science without ceaseless practice and renunciation of self, neither could he succeed in spiritual healing until self-will had been surrendered and he had paid the cost. Even then it was eternal vigilance and constant prayer. Many were called to preach to others; but mighty few were willing to heal others because of the price demanded. A man could easily cling to self-will and preach the Gospel; but in order to heal he would have to demonstrate the Gospel. This required that he be in the power of God and in God's Will, rather than in his own power and his own will. The preaching ministry was as nothing to the healing ministry. The healing of one person by the power of God was worth more than a hundred sermons delivered by a man outside of God's power.

It requires no power to diagnose the ills of others and the world. To heal the ills, however, is another matter.

A Christian healing stands for an eternal witness; a Christian sermon may stand for a word about a witness.

THE CONNECTING LINK OF LOVE

A sermon about God fades as quickly as a newspaper yarn. A living demonstration of God's power in the pain-torn body of a person carries the testimony of permanence.

The sermons Pastor Brown had preached to his flock were unremembered. These inspired no one to rise three days later in the prayer meeting and testify to their effectual power, because they had been forgotten within a few hours. But month after month and year after year members of his flock could rise and witness to the Lord's healing power. The Pastor's healing cases were remembered. The actual demonstration of his faith was vital and lasting; his expositions of that faith were all ephemeral. Verbality dies soon. Vitality lives on and on.

The verbal philosophy of theoretical knowledge has no lasting power. It is not the words of science that live, but the demonstrated fruits of science. The undemonstrated theories of theology may impress the mind for a moment. But the hearts of people are moved by a theological witness. Jesus preached and demonstrated. Without the demonstration the preachment was vain. As it was in his example so it remains to-day. There is futility in the absence of utility. Christian preachment remains unredemptive theory if it bears no fruit in the souls and lives of people.

I am certain that the redemptive influence of Pastor Brown is not so much found in his pulpit zeal and eloquence. It is the product of his faith as demonstrated in his power of prayer. When he talks about the healing ministry of Jesus he can back up his assertions with living examples out of his experience. This is ministerial adequacy, which the following case will illustrate:

In June, 1936, a woman member of the Pastor's church telephoned him. It was Sunday and she knew there was an evening prayer group which met in the church. She placed before this group a request for help on behalf of her daughter-in-law, who had given birth to a premature baby in her home. The situation was grave. The baby had been born without any one being present to assist, having been delivered within twenty minutes of the first warning.

When the doctor arrived he found the mother in a serious condition, suffering from double pneumonia. He had her rushed to the hospital, saying she had one chance in a hundred to live.

The Pastor asked the mother-in-law if she could be present at the prayer clinic that evening. But, having her hands full, she could not be with the group. So, too, the other members of the family were busy. None could attend. Pastor Brown was most insistent that the family be represented by at least one member. He explained to the mother-in-law that this would increase the effectiveness of prayer, by adding to the quantity and quality of the necessary Love.

"Here," said the Pastor, "was a situation that demanded as much Love in our prayer as could be loosed, and none of us knew the young mother. Hence the mother-in-law decided to make every effort to attend. When we gathered for the prayer clinic both she and a daughter of hers were on hand. Even before we prayed in that little upper room of the church the atmosphere was charged with the Presence of the Holy Spirit, and all of us were aware of it.

"When we gathered the young mother was dangerously ill. But the next day we learned that her improvement began during the hour we prayed. Her progress was rapid. Both mother and child came through the ordeal in what seemed a normal way. Here was a case where we were requested to pray for a stranger. It was also a case which called for a large amount of Love."

I said to Pastor Brown: "It seems rather odd to me. How did you arrive at this conclusion that you needed a member of the family present when you prayed?"

"It came to me by inspiration," replied the Pastor. "I can't explain it. It was given me at the time to know that a lot of Love was needed. I feel that the results support my feeling. A similar situation existed when Jesus raised the daughter of Jairus. He took the father and mother who had great Love for the girl, and his inner circle of disciples, Peter, James, and John. It was a tremendous moment that required vast Love, and no human beings Loved the child as much as Jesus and the parents. I have found that healing prayer is always more effective when it is motivated by great Love. This was the true inspiration, I'm sure, to surround this young mother with Love and saturate her with it."

"With this case in mind," I prompted, "and if you were going to give a theoretical explanation, how would you do it?"

"Well, therapeutic suggestion nearly always plays a part. It helps to enliven the patient's faith. Beyond this we enter the realm of imponderables. I can only say that the guidance comes to me from God. I make no attempt to understand it. I just accept it and give thanks."

Accept it. It is already present. It is not in the process of coming. It came with the Holy Spirit Whom Jesus announced. What we seek has long been seeking us. We don't evolve into it. We give up our wills and it is received. The name of this power is Love, an excellent name for God. Not an attribute of Him: a totality.

Chapter XXII . . . .

The Law Of Abiding

"Tensions Are Dropped"

RALPH Woodfield had good intentions, but his life was tangled on the side of behavior. He had studied theology and was interested in the social gospel. His desire to go into the ministry was deep and sincere. Yet this did not neutralize the confusion in his mind.

Pastor Brown deduced that Ralph's main trouble was a lack of decision, a weak commitment, and an unbalanced relationship with Jesus. The Master seemed to offer too little and demand too much. Subconsciously the precepts and examples of Jesus discouraged the young man. The precepts commanded perfection, and the examples appeared to him as an endless assortment of penalties for doing good. He was painfully conscious of his imperfections, and he quailed from the price set upon a good life. Ralph was in conflict between aspiration and execution.

He looked at the Jerusalem Road of commitment that stretched from Gethsemane to Golgotha, and seeing the Cross standing out stark and rugged against the sky, the sight unnerved him. He was not in tune with the meaning of the Cross. He was not abiding in the Lord. Nor was the Lord abiding in him. So Pastor Brown laid hold on the law of abiding as the treatment in Ralph's case best calculated to remove his fears and indecisions. "If you abide in me, and my words abide in you, ye shall ask what ye will, and it shall be done unto you."

Because of the bewilderment in his life, Ralph had not been able to sleep. He carried to bed his problems, worries, and fears. And one of his fears had now become his inability to sleep.

The Pastor gave him some suggestions on how to harmonize his life with Christ so that the Lord could become a living reality to him. Pastor Brown felt that this would entail a slow process of re-education and reconditioning. So he outlined a plan which involved a number of interviews. They were to meet once a week on a certain day and a certain hour for spiritual conversation and prayer. Said Pastor Brown:

"We prayed for a perfect cleansing and for his redemption. When Ralph came for the next appointment he brought a beaming face. He looked like a changed man. He said: 'Pastor, I've come because of our appointment. But I didn't need to see you. What you did for me was all I needed. That night I slept like a child, the first good night's sleep in six years. The fog's clearing. I'm seeing as never before. Jesus is real to me now. I'm committed to his way without fear or reservation. I'm abiding in him, and from the minute I yielded he has lived in me. It is a glorious experience, and I can show you my gratitude only in action.' It was done that promptly, and that completely."

Pastor Brown had the joy of giving the ordination prayer when Ralph Woodfield was ordained a minister of Christ, where he began to do for others what the Pastor did for him.

"This story illustrates some important facts," said Pastor Brown. "I had assumed that it would be necessary to give Ralph a lot of time because of his unusual state of mind. My intention was to tackle the job the hard, slow way, along the line of psychology, the chief virtue of which is long-suffering labor and tedious mental guidance. It was sharply revealed to me, however, that the pseudo-scientific process of extensive counselling was like ditch-digging compared to the effortless and speedy way of grace. I learned that when a man truly and sincerely desires to do the Will of God he has no need of a psychological ground boss. What he needs is an overshadowing Lord. With a man who is porous to the Divine Inflow prayer works with the speed of a purgative. The difference between the prayer approach and the counselling approach is the difference between pummelling the mind and releasing the soul. Ralph had no need of a mental spanking from me. What he needed was a spiritual baptism from Jesus. We are inclined to try to do what God alone has the power to do. And when God does it, it is often so quick and seemingly simple that it startles us."

Apparently it is just as easy for Christ to heal the body as the mind, and if the patient be open to him he can work his grace with completeness and dispatch. Take the case of Mrs. Gresham, for example. She was an outstanding leader in the Pastor's church, a woman of strong faith and Love. She sought prayer for an eye infection of long standing. The lower lid was swollen and inflamed. There were two small cysts which caused ceaseless itching. Pastor Brown put his hand upon her and prayed for a healing. The infection vanished.

Or the case of his Assistant Pastor, as another instance. David Parks had been suffering with the flu. Because of a certain inherent reticence he had not gone to a doctor. He began to run a high temperature, and became very ill. Pastor Brown prayed for him with his hand upon the man's chest. He asked God to burn out the infection. His recovery started immediately. The next day he was up and about. His lost vitality was quickly restored and he was back at work.

"When did you first discover you had healing power?"

I asked.

"My first healing was accomplished on myself," the Pastor said with a smile. "I will tell you the story.

"It was the summer of 1918. I was rushing across the street in Chicago. I was soon to board a train for Battle, Creek, Michigan. As I attempted to jump to avoid being hit by an automobile, my ankle turned, causing a bad sprain. I hobbled on to the depot platform, the pain increasing with every step. On the train I realized the seriousness of my injury. I applied cold water and rubbing in vain. Then it occurred to me that I should not be so handicapped for the task that lay ahead. The next day I was to board a troop train at Camp Custer to accompany the men to Hoboken. I was a Y.M.C.A. war work secretary, and I was the only spiritual leader on the train.

"I wanted to be at my best. So I prayed earnestly that God would heal my ankle. When we arrived at Battle Creek all the pain was gone. I had been healed."

He had opened himself to God and had received His Love, His grace, and His health.

Man cannot develop into God's Consciousness. He can get out of God's way and receive it without effort on his part.

Man cannot analyze his way to God. He can yield to Him and experience Him.

Man cannot find union between God and his natural self. God can transform the natural man into the spiritual man, and when he reaches that state, union is already established.

The spiritual way is the stressless way. Man's feverish effort has value if it puts an end to effort. Outer pressures generate inner tensions. God's plan for man is nonresistance. The key to Pastor Brown's success is that he has mastered the great secret of *letting go*.

Chapter XXIII . . . .

Mr. John Barleycorn

"Alcoholism Cured"

I WAS about twelve when I first met Mr. Barleycorn, and had my first "lost week-end." Though he made me very sick, there was something abnormally fascinating about him. He had a way of prefacing his pain with a curious sort of pleasure. It was this odd pleasure that always lured me back to him, as the proverbial dog to its vomit.

During those years of friendship with John Barleycorn, some twenty-five of them, I came to know the Barleycorn character and mission. I learned that in the beginning he was subtle and persuasive with his devotees; but that later on, when he was sure of them, he became a frank and honest realist, taking them into his confidence. He used to find a kind of vulgar joy in taunting me the morning after.

"You poor fool," he would say. "You're poisoned and sick. You're saying now you'll never touch me again. Yet deep down you know that's a lie; that I'm your master; and that you'll come to me again, battered and bloated, bleary-eyed and shaking, whining and whimpering for a drink."

John Barleycorn, man about town, former master of men, and now the master of women and youth! America's best advertized and most popular hero, now in control of stage and screen, with his trained eye on the radio! He has come far in twelve short years.

But this is not my story. My business is to tell you of the healing ministry of Pastor Brown. John Barleycorn is the father of a rapidly growing disease, which has been scientifically dubbed, *Alcoholism*. Science has named the ailment and diagnosed its victim's case. A scientific diagnosis without a scientific cure!

The question at the moment is, "Is there a cure for alcoholism?" The Pastor answers, "Yes." And he pulls out a case from his files.

She was a good Christian woman. There was no question about that. She had her husband's best interest at heart. She was sensitive about making a private revelation of his weakness. It was only with a great deal of persuasion that Pastor Brown got her to unburden her heart. When it came out it all added up to her husband's being an excessive drinker, who came home intoxicated and abusive to her and his children, a shame and a disgrace to his family and their friends.

Said Pastor Brown: "You've told him how wrong it is to drink? You've tried very hard to reform him?"

"Oh, yes, Pastor. I've done all that."

"You've backed up your position with the scriptures? You've preached many little sermons on the evils of liquor? You've done your utmost to make him yield to Jesus as his Lord and Savior? I suppose you've begged him to come to church, and have prayed to make your wish come true? No doubt you've registered your reaction every time he's come home drunken?"

She nodded.

"So you continue to scold him and quote more scripture?"

"There's nothing I haven't tried to do to help him," she said.

"Have you ever tried not to try? to turn him over to

God? to let go of him and let God have a chance at him?"

"No, Pastor, I haven't tried that yet."

"Well, then, I'm going to tell you about the method. You've already quoted the scripture, and preached, and disapproved. That failed to work. So we can drop it. You don't need to quote any more, nor preach, nor nag. All this you've tried for years, only to watch the situation grow worse. Your method has failed completely. So I'll suggest a better method. It will seem a bit unorthodox to you at first. But it will work if you'll use it. How about it?"

"I'll do my best," she promised.

"From now on, then, just stop praying for your husband and start praying for yourself. You are to seek and find and bless the good in him; and you are to criticize the weaknesses you find in yourself. Pray for your deliverance from judgment as you have never prayed before. While you are praying for yourself to be strong, love him all the more, and seek all the more to make him happy, because he is weak. From now on when he comes home intoxicated you are to ignore it and do as many loving things for him as possible. Whatever you know that would please him, do those things. Serve food he especially likes. Go out of your way to make him glad despite his evil tendencies; and don't reveal by word or deed that you are against him.

"Just remember this, he may be using drink as an escape from some intolerable condition in his home. If so find that condition and correct it. Sometimes the best-meaning Christian can be most disagreeable. Since he doesn't know the Love and beauty of Christian fellowship, it is up to you to show it to him, not by preachment, but by action. If you preach Christ to him and live the opposite before him, it will only increase his irritation. In this case he will prefer the society of the unredeemed in the tavern to that of those in his home. Live the life of Christian Love in all you say and do.

"Now I'm going to pray for both of you. Later you pray for yourself and give him to God. You may remember him in your prayers; but lovingly and thankfully, realizing that God has heard you and is bringing the right thing to pass. You may expect God to change his life, not necessarily after your will, but after His own Will. Let God change your life, so that he can see that this is much too good for him to reject any longer. He will see in you that Christ is not obnoxious or offensive; but is loving, understanding, forgiving. Nothing can draw another to Christ like a Christ-like life."

The woman agreed to do her best with this rather stiff plan of reversal. The time passed and nothing more was said. Then one day she stopped the Pastor in the aisle at church.

"Pastor Brown," she said, "a miracle has happened in our home. It has been transformed. I haven't told my husband a thing. Not once have I mentioned our conference. But do you know, I'm sure he has not touched a drop since the hour we prayed and talked. I have waited to tell you this, lest I tell it too soon. My husband rarely leaves home at night. He seems to love his home. I began doing what you told me, praying for myself and making him happy. And it worked a miracle in the whole family."

The years passed. In the Spirit, as revealed in his wife, this husband found no further occasion to seek release in liquid spirits.

Over one man and one home Mr. John Barleycorn had lost his control. He disappeared leaving the field to Jesus.

Chapter XXIV . . . .

The Arch-Demon Overcome

"Enemies Turned Into Friends"

"LOVE your enemies, bless them that curse you, do good to them which despitefully use you, and persecute you." (Matt. 5:44) Is that commandment of perfection? Can any man hope to live out so lofty a precept in the rough and tumble life of this world?

If any man does essay to Love after this fashion he will find plenty of opposition. There will be those who, unconsciously perhaps, will set themselves up as a testing block, just to see if he really means it. They will criticize, abuse, and persecute. If he be a minister he may find these self-appointed enemies of Love in his own church. If he be a layman he may find them in his own home. They will be wherever he is if he gets down to the business of being a real Christian. For this he may be duly thankful.

It is not the friends of a man's Christian Love who deepen and enrich his spiritual life. There is no great reward in Loving those who Love us. The full, ripe fruits develop out of Loving the unloving and unloveable. Nothing is so valuable to an aspiring Christian as an enemy to his Love.

While Pastor Brown related the following experience I could not help recalling instances in my own life which were similar in method and result. It is sometimes astounding to note the rapid change in an enemy's attitude after the full flame of redemptive Love has been turned on him.

A minister, by the very cloth he wears, exposes himself

as an agent of Christ. It is as though he declares, "I am a Christian, and therefore I live by the Law of Redemptive Love." He becomes a target by virtue of the position he is in. Hence a minister always has the help of enemies, who take pot shots at his private and professional life. They either make a giant out of him or a neurotic dwarf, simply by testing the quality of his proclaimed Love. In a church these are usually called the trouble-makers. As the Pastor puts it: "They are the minister's problem children. They are always dissenting, trying to divide and conquer, and to alienate the shepherd and the flock. They are skilled at stirring up strife, contention, and trouble. They seem to be agents of the Devil who have wormed their way into the sanctuary of God to prevent His Kingdom from having effect. I believe I have had my share of them." He went on:

"The woman I have in mind had a tremendous negative influence in one of my churches. She was a master at trouble-making. She could agitate a whispering campaign and manufacture a false rumor any time the unholy impulse seized her. From the outset she had shown no goodwill toward me. And I found it well-nigh impossible to Love her. It was like trying to Love Satan's most talented daughter. She never failed to join the opposition whenever any administrative matters came up. She was a confirmed pessimist, according to her own proudly given testimony.

"Sometimes, after a service, I would say to her, 'My, what a wonderful congregation we had this morning,' and she would reply, 'Yes, but what about the 200 who didn't come?' One day I suddenly realized that I was pretty well under this woman's control. My ideal of Christian Love was at stake. For I had unwittingly gotten into the habit of reacting negatively against her, and Christian Love commanded me to respond to God for her. Right at this point I made a decision. I would come out from under her control and put myself under God's control. For her evil I would return good. For her lack of Love I would give Love. I would practice holy affection toward her at all times. And I would do it secretly. It was nearing the end of December. So I decided that during January I would make her my special Love and prayer project."

"Well, Pastor," I said, "the outcome of this adventure is awaited with eager anticipation. I have had some experience with this procedure. And my feeling is that the result was a little on the amazing side."

"Yes," said Pastor Brown, "that is the word for it. Yet, why should we think it amazing. One of the best authorities has assured us that Love never fails. I began to Love her. It was a sort of long-distance method, a kind of absent treatment, and many times a day I would pray for her. Too, I would think of as many good things about her as I could. I put myself under firm discipline, checking my negative reactions instantly, and putting something positive in their place. I banked on Paul's words of advice: 'Whatsoever things are good, whatsoever things are honest, whatsoever things are just, whatsoever things are pure, whatsoever things are lovely, whatsoever things are of good report; if there be any virtue, and if there be any praise, think on these things." So it was that the month slipped away.

"In this process something mighty good was happening to me. How the actual living of Christian Love takes hold to change personality and character! How steadily the practice turns the theory into facts, living attitudes, and new habits of thought and conduct! I found myself Loving this erstwhile enemy in a way I had never felt the holy glow before. What began as a mere intellectual effort at Love was now the feeling: the imitation had become the reality. Just to think of her now set my heart to burning. My enemy was turning me into a Christian, as a dam turns a river into power. For my Love was like a river flowing, devoid of all self-effort. It was strangely beautiful and bewilderingly simple to see the immeasurable good in her. She was my friend in exile, a child of God, even as I, and she was equally Loved by Jesus."

"But Pastor," I urged, "this suspense is killing me. What happened to the woman? The process changed your life and attitude; but what about her?"

"Love never fails," he went on. "Before the month was over she, too, was changed. To watch a thing like this taking place before your eyes is to wonder why humanity has missed the Way. For here is the individual and collective answer to evil."

"I know, Pastor—but—"

"The woman began first to shake hands with people, to smile upon them, and to greet them warmly at our services. The people were surprised at the change in her and commented on it. After a Sunday service I said to her, 'What a shame it started raining as people were getting ready for church, for it has cut our attendance in half.' She replied, 'We should thank God for all those who did come.' Within six weeks she had become a living testimony in our church, influencing others redemptively by her Christian example. People would say: 'What has come over her? Her very presence makes me feel clean inside.' Yes, by the cleansing power of God's Love, she became a walking influence for good. It seemed that she had fallen in Love with Jesus all over again."

Of course every one knows that the Christian Way to face a situation where persons are involved is the Love Way. It is legitimate only to hate evil conditions which enslave persons. To Love the sinner is Christian. It is also Christian to hate the sin. But the Love Way seems the impossible way at times.

When St. Paul demands that a Christian should, "Let all that ye do be done in Love," he is seemingly counselling perfection, and this is true since the only perfection possible in the world is the capacity to express Redemptive Love. Paul calls this Love 'The bond of perfection,' and to every Christian he declares, "Walk in Love." Perhaps the reason people say that Love is impossible in certain circumstances is because they have not tried it, even as the Pastor had not tried it in this case.

"God is love." It will often prove helpful to the beginner if God and Love are used interchangeably, for Love is a synonym for God, and "He that dwelleth in Love dwelleth in God." Love in action does not destroy the Law, but fulfills it and adds the *plus*. Outside of Love obedience to Law is demanded and one grows spiritually by the legal process and discipline. Love in action brings one under the power of Grace and forgiveness. "Above all hold unfailing your love for one another, since love covers a multitude of sins." (I Peter 4:8, Revised Standard Version) Wherever the opportunity to Love is presented to you, you are favored. The enemy, offering the best opportunity, in reality is the friend in disguise.

"Some time later," said Pastor Brown, "a man decided to be a special cross for me to carry. He felt that I had made a mistake, and he began to stir up contention among my congregation. He was a man of influence, and if the poison weed of evil got into his heart sufficiently he could do much harm. People came to me in alarm, saying. 'You must do something about this man, Pastor, and you'll have to talk fast before you convince him you're right.' I knew the horizontal method of force, of argument and reason would do little good. And I knew I had found a better way, the vertical method of Love. I began to give the man a Love treatment. I bathed him in Love every day. Many times a day I prayed for him. I did not grant myself the morbid pleasure of thinking ill of him, or of making critical remarks against his back." Pastor Brown rose and walked back and forth, a faraway look in his eyes. He then lifted a foot to his chair. Leaning upon his knee he went on:

"I just kept believing in him; knowing that on the soul plane he was not an enemy but a friend; and all the time I was praying for him with affection and joy in my heart; thanking God for every splendid remembrance of him.

"Several weeks passed. Neither of us mentioned the situation. One Sunday morning, after the service, he said, 'I'd like to see you Pastor.' We moved to one side. He said, 'I suppose you know I've been critical.' My reply was, 'I know you've been unhappy about something, and I've felt sorry about it.' He said: 'Pastor, I was wrong, and I want to apologize. I've said things about you. My attitude has been unchristian.' We then prayed together. We parted as good friends. We have remained good friends."

Here were two instances dealing with human relationships. In both cases there was a dangerous rift. Could any power less than Christian Love have healed these wounds?

While this Christian Love seems impossible where enemies are concerned, we see the fallacy of such a belief in these examples. We do not use the Love Way because we do not choose to use it. It wounds our ego and hurts our pride to return good for evil, to go the other mile, or to turn the other cheek. It isn't that we can't do it, for God has given us the capacity. We do not want to do it, because the Enemy has control of us. It is an irritant to our vanity to respond to God for one who despitefully uses us. It lays a whip-lash on our egotism to Love those who are unloving toward us. But every such stripe inflicted on the ego is struck in the emancipation of the soul. "Beloved, let us love one another; for love is of God; and every one that loveth is born of God, and knoweth God. He that loveth not knoweth not God; for God is love. He that saith he is in the light, and hateth his brother, is in darkness even until now. He that loveth his brother abideth in the light, and there is none occasion of stumbling in him."

The Christian Way is the Love Way. Man has the capacity to follow that Way. To Love not and still claim the title of Christian is hypocrisy, sham, and pretense. The Christian Way compels us to Love or brands us as hypocrites. There is profit in going through the fires of aroused egotism as we "walk in love."

"There was still another person in our church," said Pastor Brown, "whom I allowed to test me to the breaking point. If there was any trouble brewing, any malicious gossip set in motion, I could nearly always put my finger on its source. This man for some reason known only to himself was out to destroy my ministry. He made no bones about it. He employed no subtlety in letting people know that he was out to get me. He could and would quote scripture like a seminary student. In his behavior his hypocrisy was undisguised. All the weaknesses that he had in himself he condemned in others. He preached morality and religion in direct opposition to the life he lived. He was a pathetic neurotic, filled with unhappy phobias. In his character and personality was none of the beauty and sweetness of Christian Love. He was as hard as pig-iron, a Christian with no Christ, cold, cynical, puritanical.

"One day my wife said to me, when I was greatly worried over his latest falsehood, 'Why don't you act like a Christian toward him, and turn the Love of Jesus on him?' I had to admit that I didn't want to Love him. He was my Christian Waterloo. Against him my religion was falling to pieces. He was indeed my enemy, and unless I could obey the commandment of Jesus I had to confess that my Christianity was in name only, for no man could be Christian and resent instead of Love an enemy. There was no such a thing as Christian resentment against persons, Christian hate against other children of God, no matter how misguided they were. As it stood, this man unloved by me, made my claims and my ministry a burlesque. With this unloved enemy sitting in my congregation I was robed in the dark cloth of counterfeit. I was preaching to others a doctrine I refused to live. 'If ye fulfil the royal law according to the Scripture, thou shalt Love thy neighbor as thyself.' Bowed in shame and weakness, I had to tell my wife that I was not without enmity toward this man. I had no desire to practice Christian Love toward him. My will was equal to the turning of Love on others, but not on him.

"My wife persisted: 'You know what the Love of God has done before. The greater the enemy the greater the Love needed to overcome him. An enemy is not more powerful than the Love of Christ. He Loves this man. He can express his Love through you if you'll let him. This may be your very chance to redeem him. His need is your chance. If you fail here your failure is everywhere. If you succeed here how can you miss your reward?' She poured oil on my fire.

"There rose before me the Apostle Paul, his words searing my soul: 'Let all bitterness, and wrath, and anger . . . and evil speaking, be put away from you, with all malice.' And this was climaxed out of the mouth of James, 'The wrath of man worketh not the righteousness of God.' Still I had to shake my head in defeat, adding the weakness of self-defense to the weakness of disobedience.

"I told my wife that while Love would work redemption in an ordinary person, it would not do so in a character of this kind. But she insisted that the man's redemption was God's responsibility and my possibility. I was not obligated to redeem him; but I was commanded to Love him redemptively and to forgive him as a Christian and a man. She brought me face to face with defeat or victory. I had to decide. It was a crisis in my life and ministry. Against the rock of this man I would make or break. When the conflict subsided I made the decision on my knees before God. By His grace and the strength of Jesus I would do my best to forgive and Love as a Christian."

The Pastor's study grew still with his pause.

"I began hesitantly and feebly," he said, "to turn Love on him. I tried not to judge him by the obvious outer appearances. I tried to think of him constructively and creatively, as Jesus who has gone to the Cross on his behalf. I began to thank God mentally for him, and mentally to thank Him for leading him to my church. Laboriously I tried to write his faults in the sands, and to seek out the virtues in him. So my discipline moved into days and weeks. My prayers for the man rose ceaselessly from the burning altar of my heart.

"There came a day when prayer was easy and Love was real. With this I was no longer concerned as to whether he was changed or not. That was God's concern. I had arrived at peace in my soul. My attitude toward the man was transformed. And his was transformed toward me. My arrival became his arrival. We are where we are because of what we are. The outer condition is but a reflection of an inner state.

"Eight years have gone. Not once in all that time has the man caused me any difficulty. When I had really Loved him and had found peace, he said to me at the door of the church: 'Pastor, that was a powerful sermon you preached this morning. It seemed especially for me.' And that was the first time he had ever made a remark that savored of compliment to me. So I have come to realize that in practice and experience Love and prayer make all things work together for good. God puts these powers at our disposal, and we can elect to use them or refuse them. Either one is mightily effective; but when the two go together, the results are often astonishing, and are always redemptive."

Chapter XXV . . . .

Jesus The Savior At Work

"Dementia Praecox Overcome"

"IT WAS on Saturday," said Pastor Brown, "when I received a long distant telephone call. It was a request to leave my home here in Chicago the following day for the Gulf of Mexico, to meet a man who was suffering from a mental disorder which was described as scientifically incurable. It was believed that I might be able to help the man through counsel and prayer.

"I felt that God was in the call. So I agreed to make the trip. I made arrangements for some one to occupy my pulpit on Sunday evening, and I boarded a train on Sunday afternoon. Not until I arrived did I know the nature of the man's condition. It was then that I was introduced to a very interesting case of dementia praecox. The man had been under the care of some of the best psychiatrists in America, and had spent several years in mental hospitals without being cured.

"When I saw the patient my heart went out to him in a strong feeling of Love. We had fellowship for a few days. I prayed for him many times; but could observe no corrective change in him. I also counselled with him in the absence of noticeable results. Then one day, while we were standing together in front of the fireplace, I fired a pointblank question at him: 'Tell me this. Have you ever honestly and decisively accepted the Lord Jesus Christ as your personal Savior?' I was surprised that I had blurted this out in such a blunt, crusader fashion to a man I had just met and scarcely knew.

"He turned slowly and looked me squarely in the eye. I could feel the searching penetration of his gaze. At the moment I could not tell whether I was condemned or approved in his sight. Then I saw his eyes fill with new light. I can describe it only as a light of concentrated hope. He raised his hand and let it fall on my back with a thud that shook my whole body. He almost shouted the words: 'That's exactly it. That's what I need and want.' My heart began to beat rapidly. I was filled with gratitude.

"Within the next half hour I had explained the Christian plan of salvation, and had succeeded in leading this man to an acceptance of Jesus as his Lord and Savior. Nothing more nor less than this had ever been needed. His old habits began to fall away, slowly at first, but surely. Others were drawn to him who could help him with advice and prayer. Although it was not an instantaneously complete recovery, time worked with him, and a real peace came. Harmony returned to his home, and he became a useful citizen once more. Seven years later I met him and found his recovery almost 100% complete."

From Chicago to the Gulf of Mexico! Surely that was a sacrificial journey. But what a great reward! A captive soul set free! A mind healed! A broken man made new!

In this connection the case of Thomas Smith is reported by the Pastor. He had heard of Pastor Brown through friends. So when he came with his wife to Chicago to spend a few days of their vacation they got in touch with the Pastor. Their home was in Iowa. Thomas himself came from a well known family in Chicago, all of whom were outstanding and devoted Christians.

For twenty years the man had been a mental case. He

had had eight major mental breakdowns, each one of which had committed him to a mental hospital. He had been a patient in these hospitals in different parts of the country. He related his experiences to the Pastor, and the memories were obviously horrible. His body still bore the marks of brutality.

When Mr. Smith visited Pastor Brown he was in a pitiful condition. He feared he was on the verge of another break, and the prospect of it was a grievous torment to him. There followed several visits in which the Pastor prayed for him, counselled with him, and gave him relaxing treatments. Once his wife came with him, and seemed almost pathetically eager for his recovery. She urged him to remain in Chicago, while she returned to their home.

He attended the Pastor's services and went to his study for frequent interviews. Apparently there was no progress being made. But the prayer of importunity continued. Often he would weep and declare: "Oh, I wish I could get well. I hope God will heal me. I don't want to be this way."

His attitudes were chiefly negative. He read the Scriptures hungrily, and everything else of a religious nature. Whenever he came upon a passage in the Bible, such as, "Believe on the Lord Jesus Christ and thou shalt be saved," he would be thrown into conflict and self-enquiry, wondering if he really *believed*.

Because of this the Pastor forbade him to read the Bible or any other religious literature. Instead he set him to reading light fiction and mystery stories. He was sent to exciting motion pictures, and was given other occupations to divert his mind from himself.

By and by Pastor Brown began to train him in prayer, urging him to pray in a positive rather than a negative vein; to thank God for his blessings rather than to plead with Him for release. The man earnestly tried to cooperate, doing as best he could with the Pastor's suggestions.

RECOVERY

He returned to his home five weeks from the day he arrived in Chicago, alert and ready to start work again.

The last prayer meeting he attended in the Pastor's church he gave his testimony. In part he said: "I can never forget this church and the glorious experience I have had with your Pastor. His heart is filled with the Love of Christ. He has compassion for all who are in need, and patience. I praise God, and will remember you all in my prayers of thanksgiving."

It was a fitting end after so many years of vexation and misery.

Chapter XXVI . . . .

Holy Spirit vs. Unholy Spirits

"Alcoholics Anonymous"

IN DRINKING, as in crime, there is a caste system. One type of criminal pretends to sicken at another type. So do the social drinkers assume to look down upon the anti-social guzzlers. In this system of caste there seems to be three main levels. At the top are the social drinkers who are called "smart people." It is the upper crust in the boozing society. These "smart people" are the aristocracy of the wine bibbers and cocktail tipplers. Out of this drinking aristocracy the second level is formed. These are called the "barflies." The barfly is a drinker who has killed pride. Out of the barflies the third level is spawned. These are called the "tavern bums." The tavern bum has put off honor.

The bibbing society is like a school system in reverse. The grades are down instead of up. It runs from a thin ditch at the top to a deep gutter at the bottom. The gutter grows out of the ditch. The barflies and tavern bums are the unwanted offspring of "smart people."

"Drinking," wrote Dr. E. Stanley Jones in his huge little book, *The Way,* "is the refuge of the weak; it is crutches for lame ducks." Dr. Jones' truth and humor can bite like bonded whiskey. "Crutches for lame ducks."

He might have substituted *spirits* for *drinking.* Hence,

the sentence, "spirits is a refuge of the weak." The Apostle Paul offered a better refuge for weaklings: "Likewise, the SPIRIT helpeth our infirmities." This refuge becomes release. When weak men put on the armour of SPIRIT they become strong. When strong men put on the shabby cloak of *spirits* they become weak.

Alcoholics Anonymous have discovered that the surest cure now for the victim of *spirits* is SPIRIT.

As we look at these three levels of "lame ducks" or drinkers, we can see that the so-called social bibbers, or "smart people," are the parents of alcoholics. Hence they are the breeders of indescribable crime, ruin, suffering, tragedy, broken homes and broken hearts.

The following case will illustrate in a mild way what it means to be an alcoholic. It will also demonstrate the Source of healing.

As a rule the confirmed alcoholic is a nervous, sensitive type of person, hounded by inferiority and some unhappy frustrations. Inner conflicts are never resolved because their source is never corrected. The war within him grows out of an over-demanding conscience, on the one hand, and over-developed appetites, on the other hand.

The sufferings of alcoholics are of a secret nature. They are feared because misunderstood, and they become the objects of judgment, the sharp shafts of which should not be turned upon them, the helpless victims, but upon the Addiction business which is the real villain in the piece. The war between conscience and appetite is a private one. Both are insatiable, and the clash between them ends in the search for relief and release. When the victims of this insatiable "civil war" turn to spirits for intoxication it is comparatively easy for them to become alcoholics, drinking themselves into a state of insensibility, and for a brief period they are able to escape from the vexations of their inner war.

Following a liberating spree there comes a more subtle

suffering, and one a thousand times worse. Here they experience remorse, guilt, shame. The relief is again intoxication. It is a vicious circle which leads toward the total loss of self-respect and honor, the blunting of conscience and general personality destruction.

Oddly enough the confirmed alcoholic, like the confirmed criminal, is responsive to religious persuasion if properly presented to him. He is receptive to prayer, if the one praying is genuine, nonpossessive, tolerant, understanding, and compassionate. He is an easy prospect for Jesus because of the nature and greatness of his need. Because of this fact Alcoholics Anonymous, by employing a well-arranged religious approach, is saving drunkards by the thousands.

Pastor Brown is familiar with this salvage program and cooperates with it. He knows that once the alcoholic experiences the intoxication of the Holy Spirit he will never again take a false refuge in unholy spirits. Alcoholics Anonymous is not a church, but it has prepared thousands of men and women for church membership. It has cleaned up their lives so thoroughly as to make them acceptable to the Christian Church. Nor have these former drunks later soiled the skirts of respectable Christians in close contact. In fact, they have brought a new vitality into church circles, a new tone and quality of Christian fellowship.

Surely it is a wonderful thing for a person who has been in the hell and gutter of alcoholism so to regain his Selfhood that the doors of the Church open to him. It is a miracle of Grace.

As a young woman said to me one day after I had addressed a street meeting: "You speak too easily. There are many roads leading into this skidrow sewer of life; but the one-away road you offer as a way out is rather remote and abstract. Don't you think?" She had been given all the advantages of education. She spoke with intelligence, and her words commanded attention. She was a finished alcoholic. At twenty-six she was burned out with vice and dissipation. She was caught in the skidrow sewer of which she spoke. My reply was:

"Only by the miracle of Love and Grace through Jesus Christ can you get out of here. Many paths lead down. He is the only path that will lead you up again, and restore you to life and decency. For you he is the Great Physician. You will find no other. Break at his feet in abject surrender and he will lead you up and out." I saw the miracle of surrender and redemption performed on that soggy spot, which turned a slave to spirits into a missionary of the SPIRIT.

As a national pastime liquor drinking has now permeated every nook and corner of the nation, and has gathered in converts from all classes and practically all ages. Consequently we may look forward to the disease of alcoholism as assuming the proportions of a minor plague, similar to criminality. The nation now has the cost of five million active criminals on its taxation shoulders, and there is perhaps an equal number of men and women in the grip of liquor. These blind followers of the blind are a national liability.

Since an orthodox science can do little to heal the confirmed alcoholic, which, like criminality, is a disease of the conscience, and since applied religion has demonstrated its power to heal these victims, the nation is not left without hope on the corrective side, though seemingly it is helpless on the prevention side. The following case out of Pastor Brown's file will illustrate the power of religion to redeem the habitual drunkard.

"The woman was a good Christian," he said, "and I wondered what was on her heart when she telephoned me and asked to see me. I went to her home to hear the tragic story. It concerned her son-in-law, a slave to liquor. She told of the ruin he had brought to himself and family.

She wanted to know if anything could be done to help such a man. He and his family lived out of town. So I told her that we could pray about it, since time and space were no barriers against the Holy Spirit.

"I doubt if ever two persons prayed more earnestly. My heart was filled with Love for this unfortunate drunkard and his suffering family. The woman wept because of her great concern and heartbreak. We prayed for the redemption of the man's soul, knowing that all needful things would follow this act of grace; that it would take away the desire for liquor, and turn the degrading process into a program of decency and dignity. With all the faith and Love we could muster the man's life was committed to God.

"Sometime later the woman reported the result. That very week after we had prayed, the man was walking on the street when he met another man and struck up an acquaintance. They began to talk about drinking, and the stranger told him something of the work being done by Alcoholics Anonymous, and of the many chapters that had been organized all over the country. He spoke of the thousands who had been cured through this missionary band of ex-drinkers.

"The son-in-law was inspired by what he heard. His interest was aroused and he joined the group immediately. From the day he put in his membership he has not touched a drop. The years have passed only to confirm the permanency of his recovery.

"He in turn has become a missionary for Alcoholics Anonymous, and began to lead others to the unfailing Source of release. Too, he became a highly respected citizen in his community, acclaimed for his works of charity and civic enterprise. The thing most appreciated by his wife was a new habit he had formed. Whereas he had sought release in the taverns through evil spirits, he now found that release in the Holy Spirit."

RECOVERY

Pastor Brown commented:

"Here is an example of another way in which God can answer prayer. In this instance He used as His vehicle one of the chapters of Alcoholics Anonymous, which has been such a blessing to so many prisoners of drink."

There is always an open door for the prisoner of habit. "I am the door, by me if any man enter in he shall be saved, and shall go in and out, and find pasture." That door is never closed to a man or a nation. It is a Door of invitation to all, no matter how far down in the scale they have sunk. "Come and see."

Chapter XXVII . . . .

God's Supply For Man's Needs

"The Housing Problem Met"

THE HOUSING shortage that developed during and after the war will long be remembered. It became the habit of the voice of doubt to declare, "Obtaining a place to live is out of the question." Over against this denial the voice of faith could always affirm, "There is a place to live, a supply to match the demand, if the need and the supply can somehow meet."

Praying for a place to live is a perfectly legitimate use of the prayer magnet. Critics of prayer may hold otherwise, saying: "If you pray for a place to live and obtain the answer to this prayer you make God a respecter of persons and a coddler of pets. For under the present housing conditions if you obtain a house by means of prayer, you must assume that you are occupying a place that is equally or even more needed by some one else. Hence God is especially favoring one person at the expense of another."

This brand of logic and reasoning, however, is shallow and superficial. In the act of prayer there are always three factors, except in the purely devotional prayers. These are the need, the Source, and the supply. A praying person with a need must assume the corresponding supply, and exercise faith in God to bring the need and the supply together. When they meet, that particular supply belongs to that particular need. There is no favoritism shown and nothing gained at some one else's expense. It is simply the application of the law of harmony and synchronization. On the other hand, management, manipulation, fixing, and conniving in order to get possession is as unnatural as God's way is natural. Which all goes to show that to secure a house *without* prayer is much more likely to be a result of favoritism, of injustice and liable to throw the divine, harmonious relationship of need and supply out of balance than when it is secured in the proper way. When anything is done in God's way it is always done the right way. And one of the sure methods of obtaining possessions correctly is to work under God's Will and approval. He labors in vain who labors for self. His labor bears fruit who labors for soul.

In the following series of demonstrations by means of prayer Pastor Brown begins by saying:

"Things happen so fast and gloriously for those of us who are learning to let God work through us, especially for our young people, that we are beginning to expect great things, for we have witnessed in many areas the marvelous results of prayer. Nor has this made any of us more result-minded and less-God-minded.

"When the servicemen had begun to return, some to wives they had left and some to wives just taken, they found it difficult to live with their in-laws. They were greatly in need of apartments or homes of their own. But seemingly no homes and apartments were available to any of them. We took these matters to God in prayer.

"These prayer projects began when Mrs. Robert Cooksey, in much distress, called me one evening and asked if she could come to our home. After arriving she said: 'Pastor, I simply have to have a place to live. My baby is due in three months, and we'll need our own apartment. We've looked everywhere and have done everything we know. But we can't find a place. I wonder if you'll pray with me about it?' And I replied: 'Of course I will, Dorothy. I'll pray and I know this that if God wants you to have your own apartment He will have a place for you on time.' Then I prayed with her. Two days later she and her husband made a deposit on an apartment directly across the street from our church, and they moved in a week later. This was most convenient for the Cooksey family, as Mr. Cooksey was our choir director. We were grateful to have him nearby.

"Some weeks later I called for them at four in the morning and drove them to the hospital. Ten days later I drove them back home with little Virginia Ann.

"After moving into their apartment they told another couple who were members of our church about this answer to prayer. Mr. and Mrs. Berglund were also in need of a place to live. One day they marched into my office. They sat there chatting away about inconsequentials. But I knew there was something more serious on their hearts, and I told them to come out with it. 'Pastor, we've come because we want you to pray that we find a place to live. The house we have has been sold. It's necessary that we find another very soon. We're willing to buy or to rent.' Then I prayed with them. I prayed that God would lead them to the place they were supposed to have, whether it be an apartment for them to rent or a house for them to buy. We put no string upon it; but stated the problem and turned it over to God, believing He would answer the prayer in His own time and way.

"In less than a week they had the house which they decided to buy. It was located a block away from where they were living. When they had been settled they invited Mrs. Brown and me to the home and we had a little prayer of dedication with them.

"Shortly after this a number of us were together when Mrs. Berglund told how God had answered this prayer within a week. Mr. and Mrs. Cooksey declared that this was nothing, that 'when Pastor prayed for us we got an apartment in two days.' Whereupon David Parks, our Assistant Pastor, spoke up and said: 'Well, that's nothing either. We got our apartment within an hour.

"He then told how he and his wife lived some twenty miles from the church at the time he had been called to take his position. They had looked all over for a place and found nothing. I had been praying that something would be found by the time he arrived on our staff. When he and I entered the church at nine on the morning he came to take up his duties, I picked up the mail. The first letter I opened was from a woman who was leaving the community. She had scarcely gotten settled in her lovely apartment for which she had purchased the furnishings, when she had to leave. I handed the letter to Mr. Parks, and said, 'Dave, here's your apartment.' And within the hour arrangements were being made to secure the apartment and shortly after, they moved in.

"By now the young people in the church were becoming quite excited, and soon Mr. and Mrs. Howard Curry asked for prayer. They too were in need of an apartment. Howard had recently returned from overseas where he had been wounded. They were living with their in-laws and the situation was acute. They could find nothing. So we prayed about it. A few days later we made the discovery that one of our members had moved his family to Washington, D. C., and had left a furnished apartment which they were willing to sublet. It filled the need perfectly and they moved in.

"But the most interesting example of all was that of Mr. and Mrs. Ray Monson. Ray is a precious lad. He became a Christian and I baptized him when he was a little fellow. He had just been discharged from the Air Corps after returning from Italy. He went to Nebraska to be married. Then he brought his wife to Chicago. But there was no place for them to live that they could find. They tried to live first with one relative and then with another. Such an arrangement was naturally unsatisfactory for a bride and groom.

"So after church one Sunday night they told me about their problem, and asked me to pray. I asked them if I should pray then or make an appointment for a later time. They suggested the following evening, Christmas Eve. On the following evening Mrs. Brown and I, in keeping with our traditional custom, entertained our young people around the fireplace. So it had been agreed that we would pray together sometime during the evening.

"By some peculiar trick of our minds we met as planned on Christmas Eve, but we had completely forgotten our prayer project. The day following Christmas I called on a widow whose husband I had recently buried. She told me she was leaving in a few days for a trip to Florida to be gone a month, and that when she returned she thought perhaps she might rent a room to some nice person. Promptly I asked, 'Wouldn't you like to rent it to a nice bride and groom?' Her response to the idea was immediate. The next day Ray saw her about it, and the newlyweds were ready to move into a good apartment. The widow and the young people fell in love with one another at first sight. The arrangement had the blessing of God upon it from the outset.

"It was only then that we realized that we had not prayed. It had not been necessary. God knew the need and the desire in our hearts. He fulfilled His promise, Isa. 65:24, 'And it will come to pass, that before they call, I will answer; and while they are yet speaking, I will hear.' On the following day Ray came to see me in order that we might pray together and give thanks to God for His mindfulness and Love. I deeply appreciated this quality in Ray, for only on rare occasions do people return, like the one leper out of ten blessed, to give thanks.

"While the lad was with me I had reason to go to the bank. I suggested that he ride along. As we stood at the Teller's cage, one of our deacons, Edgard C. Christensen, stepped up to us and said, 'You're the very ones I want to see.' He introduced us to the man with whom he was talking, a building contractor, and the deacon had been asking him if he could give Ray employment. They had previously discussed the idea of Ray's becoming a carpenter's apprentice under the G I Bill of Rights. The two of them were wondering how they were going to arrange an interview with Ray when we came into the bank and the object of their wonderment stood before them. When my business was over, the interview was over. The job was secured for Ray, and he has been working ever since. He loves the work. His employer is a consecrated Christian, and a leading official in a near-by church. How perfectly God can make everything work together for those who Love Him! When Ray came back to give thanks for one blessing God gave him this double portion.

"All this creates and deepens our fellowship. Similarity of demonstration acts as cement, welding these young people into a closer bond of Love and faith. And the synchronization so obvious in these cases is a beautiful example of the miraculous yet natural way in which the Father works among those who Love Him."

As Pastor Brown concluded his series of illustrations I was reminded that in each case everything was done that could humanly be done before these persons resorted to prayer. Their extremities had become God opportunities.

Chapter XXVIII . . . .

From Dollars To Duty

"The Senior Partner At Work"

"NOW, Pastor," I said, "I want to touch upon a delicate issue. In order to run a church, like everything else, money is needed. But just as there is a reluctance on the part of people to talk about mental sickness, so there seems to be a sort of understood taboo in regard to associating the dollar with Deity, money with religion. On the other hand many ministers believe in wearing out shoe leather in fund-raising campaigns, and in expending persuasive energy from their pulpits to this end. What is your attitude in this connection?"

Pastor Brown was not opposed to the method of wearing out shoe leather and the vocal cords; but he felt that it was perfectly legitimate also to wear the cloth a little at the knees when funds were needed. He then recounted the following example, and the reader will agree that there was a financial need of the most urgent kind. We may let the Pastor tell his own story:

"For many years our church needed a new basement floor. The old wooden floor was in a process of decay. The room was essential. Here we had our Bible school, youth activities, and our mid-week prayer services.

"The walls were beaverboard as was the ceiling. There was a kitchen and a couple of discarded gas ranges and a sink. When we had no coal to heat the large room for our prayer meetings we would resort to the kitchen and light the two gas ovens; and there in the fragrance, if it could be called such, of escaping gas from numerous leaks, we would thank God that we were able to bear up.

"There were certain advantages. With chilled bodies and stiff feet no one was inclined to be long-winded in verbal prayer. We sang to the accompaniment of a doleful little portable organ which sat in front of one of the stoves. The memories of that little group holding a prayer meeting will never fade. It was spiritual heroism at its best.

"One bitter cold night as we worshipped and prayed and suffered together in the kitchen, I laid it upon the hearts of the brave little company to try to vision a new basement room, rebuilt and just as perfect as it ought to be. I told them to dream it even as they shivered and choked with smarting eyes, and that if we could see it clearly enough when we prayed, maybe the Lord would agree with our dream and bring it into reality. At this point in the unburdening of my soul, some one opened the kitchen door that we might get a breath of living air. He may have thought the gas fumes were affecting my mind and reasoning powers.

"But the need was desperate and it called for desperate methods. When we walked across the floor in the main room we often stumbled into holes. We were carrying a mortgage of $7600.00 and what was left from an accumulation of unpaid bills which amounted to $2000.00. Under such circumstances how could a new floor be installed. But regardless of our misgivings we called a joint meeting of the trustees and finance committee, and put the burden of our prayer and vision before them. When all the details had been worked out we knew the cost of remodelling the whole basement. It would cost $1500.00. To the men this figure was out of the question.

Then as if inspired I said, 'Well, it is just as easy to pray for $1500.00 as it is to pray for $300.00 or $100.00.'

"Following that remark there was a vast silence. But by and by the committee came into perfect agreement. With this we prayed about it earnestly, laying the matter before God, telling Him we wanted to do only His Will, and to indicate His Will by the response or lack of it when we put the issue to the church membership.

"On the morning we presented the problem to the church and asked for an expression, $868.00 was subscribed on the spot. When the final count was in, it amounted to $3000.00. The whole basement was done over, a beautiful streamlined room with paneling celotex walls and ceiling, interspersed with black masonite. A new kitchen came into reality with all modern equipment, so that to-day we have a well-appointed whole lower floor. It was less than a year from the idea to the realization and dedication. In this time every penny was paid from the pockets of the parishoners, and in small amounts. The Lord favored our vision and our prayer, even as we dreamed and shivered together."

Chapter XXIX . . . .

The Healing Power of Light

"Influenza Vanishes"

INVISIBLE light lies all about us. It is invisible only because its rate of vibration is greater than the capacity of our eyes to see, even as sound fills all space around the earth without being heard. By means of radio receiving sets the inaudible sounds are modified, their vibrations lowered to the capacity of the ear to hear them. In a dark room there is light which cannot be seen. But to become aware of this light by means of faith is to become receptive to its therapeutic value.

In the healing ministry of Pastor Brown there is an exceptionally fine example of how a sick man can make use of invisible light, focus it to his purpose by means of conscious faith, and in a comparatively short time receive the blessing of recovered health. We may let the Pastor himself relate the story of his own healing.

"Several years ago," he said, "I caught the flu. I should have been in bed, according to good sense and medical advice, and I should have ignored the interests of other people until my own best interest had been served. But it seemed that the pressures of duty were greater than ever before. I did spend as much time in bed as I felt I could; but I had to preach twice each Sunday; I had to conduct our mid-week service; and during my illness I had been called upon to hold four funeral services. But finally at the close of a Sunday morning service I came home immediately and went to bed, completely exhausted. I didn't see how I could get ready for the evening service and preach again that night.

"While lying in bed that afternoon the words of Jesus crept silently into my consciousness, 'I am the Light of the world.' It seemed that immediately I associated those words with my condition. The therapeutic value of light occurred to me. The medical profession had adopted the heat lamps, ultra-violet rays, and so on, and people were being urged to remain out-of-doors where they would be exposed to the sunlight.

"I thought of the incandescent light. It had a certain rate of vibration; the ultra-violet rays were of a higher rate; and the higher up we go in light frequency the more invisible and powerful become the rays, until we reach the X-rays and ultimately the cosmic rays, the most invisible and powerful of all, which even penetrate the earth's surface.

"Now Jesus was saying that he is the light. If I were to follow this graduated process of thinking I would reach an inevitable conclusion, namely, that the vibrations of Jesus were much higher, more invisible, more powerful, and more penetrating than any of the other rays, for his light was spiritual, the most invisible and most powerful element in the world, which, if it could be focussed to the need, would surely act as a wonderful therapeutic agent. It would be wonderful if I could lie here in bed and actually absorb with a fixed purpose the rays of him who said, 'I am the Light of the world,' and be completely healed of the infection in my body.

"With the theory came the practice. I had nothing to lose by such an experiment, and I had the possibility of regaining my health. I therefore stretched out in the bed with my arms extended in the form of a cross and imagined I was lying on the warm sands of an expansive and extensive seashore with the sun bathing me in its warm, mellow rays, penetrating every cell of my body. Then I shifted from imagination to affirmation of Jesus and accepted his promise, 'Lo, I am with you always.' I now declared that the Son's rays were under me, above me, around me, and within me, touching every atom in my being, dissolving all infected areas and establishing vital health.

"My faith-sustained affirmation became in time an inner sense of conviction, of *knowing*. I knew that the Christ rays were more powerful than a therapeutic lamp, than the sun, or even the cosmic rays. I knew they were powerful enough to consume every bit of poison in my system. So I lay in that position for an hour, knowing that 'The Light of the world' was accomplishing his perfect work, and it seemed as though I could feel the warmth of his rays.

"At the end of the treatment I was completely well as far as feeling could determine. And as far as I know all the infection had been dissolved in my body and had been replaced by a healthy condition. I got up and prepared my evening sermon. I preached that night with greater freedom and ease than usual, nor had I ever felt better in my life. My soul as well as my body had been effected. The warmth and radiation of the Love of Jesus had gone clear through my being. The old conditions had passed away and I had emerged from my experience as a new person."

This process may be a trifle difficult for an orthodox scientist; and the rigidly systematized philosopher may have a psychological explanation in order to rule out the idea of Christ. But if by its fruit we can know the tree, then by the same token can Pastor Brown know the Source of this interesting cure.

There is no need to argue with a man who *knows* the

truth as it is revealed, not by the intellectual process of deduction or induction, but by direct inspiration under the guidance of the Holy Spirit. No intellect that seeks may ever have this kind of knowledge. Only the intellect that surrenders its false position as master, and assumes its true position as servant, may ever know the truth that goes beyond the relative and touches the absolute.

The Pastor's only answer to the skeptical here is, "I did as you have read, and the result was as stated." It is the answer of the blind man, "All I know is that I was blind and now I see."

Chapter XXX . . . .

Christ The Employer

"Unemployment Problems Met"

THIS is a good example of simple faith, the kind of trust that makes prayer most surely effective. It is typical of many such problems the Pastor dealt with back in the Depression days.

During those years scores of persons sought him for help concerning employment. Seldom did he know of an available job to fit the need. But he did know that faith and work go together; and that if an unemployed man would trust his whole life to God he would be in tune with the work that belonged to him, and for which he had been prepared.

"The jobs these men were seeking," said Pastor Brown, "were seeking them. I did not know where the job was. But God knew. So if a man requested prayer I would ask God to reveal the job and fill the need. Most of the men who sought me were of simple, uncorrupted faith. My desire was to put their idle hands in the hands of Jesus, and let him bring the man and the job together."

I asked the Pastor if the men with whom he prayed had found the employment they needed.

"Over a period of two years," he replied, "I do not know of a single one who failed to secure a job. Usually it was done quickly, within a few days."

As an example the Pastor told of the case of his housekeeper, a negro woman, and her unemployed son.

"She knew that people came to pray with me about jobs," he said. "She had heard us talk of the jobs obtained through prayer. So being a woman of faith, unspoiled by too much learning, she had me pray for her son. He had been idle for a long time, and they were in need of his salary. He was willing and able to work. But though he sought continuously he found no job. The following day she had her son see me. I questioned him about his faith."

"Where do you think God is?"

He thought that God was remote. His eyes looked up and out. He was thinking in terms of a distant place out beyond his reach.

"You think God is out yonder beyond the stars?"

He nodded.

"You are partly right," agreed the Pastor. "God is infinite. He is as far away as your mind can stretch. But just because He is infinite He is also as near as breathing and hands and feet. He is now right here with us. Can you believe this?"

He said that he did believe it.

"Well, then, what do you think God is like?" The man thought for a moment and his face took on a wistful look. He described God as like a big man, soft of hands, with which to caress His Children.

"You're right," said Pastor Brown. "Don't lose that picture of God. It is a perfect description of Him. He is a God of Love, and He Loves you with all his heart. He Loves you as though you were the only person in the world for whom His Son died. You do believe this?"

The man believed it. And the Pastor asked:

"What do you think God is able to do for you?"

"He can do anything," was the reply.

"Anything?"

"Yes. Just anything."

"Do you mean that God is able to get you a job?"

"Yes," he affirmed.

"You must be sure of this," said Pastor Brown. "Suppose you had a rich uncle, and he was here now, sitting with us, and he loved you dearly, as his only relative, with all his heart, and he was able because of his wealth and influence to do anything for you that you desired. Don't you think he would find a job for you?"

"I'm sure he would," he answered.

"Then it seems to me," continued the Pastor, still working to stimulate the man's faith, "that if God is here right now, and He Loves you with all His heart, and He is able to give you a job, all we need to do is ask Him for it."

The man admitted the logic in this deduction.

"It was a great joy to pray for and with this man," said Pastor Brown. "His quick trust and undisguised faith were wholesome. I was in the presence of a clear soul, the like of which I had rarely seen in an educated and sophicticated man. Because of this I knew in advance that our prayer would be answered. He thanked me and left. As he reached the door I reminded him to walk hand in hand with Jesus, for Jesus was going to lead him to the job he needed. In less than one hour my telephone rang. The call was for our housekeeper, the man's mother. When she hung up the receiver she reported that her son had just been hired as a night watchman in a garage. God had not delayed His response to this man's childlike trust and responding heart.

"That happened ten years ago. But in memory it is still fresh. I have often drawn upon the demonstration for the enrichment of my own faith," the Pastor concluded. I asked:

"What message would you leave with those readers who may also wish to become effectual in prayer?" He quoted a famous passage from St. Paul: "I am crucified with Christ, nevertheless I live, yet not I, but Christ liveth in me: and the life which I now live in the flesh I live by the faith of the Son of God, who loved me, and gave himself for me."

"The discipline of crucifixion," said Pastor Brown, "is an essential factor. It means the elimination of all those unredemptive attitudes, motives, and actions which destroy dependence on God, and which alienate the supply from the need.

"Thus to be dead is to live the new and abundant life, because it is Christ doing the living within, motivating the heart, guiding the mind, and enlivening all the faculties for his own expression. The new life is the life of Faith, Hope and Love in the Son of God who Loved us, and who gave his life for us."

Chapter XXXI . . . .

Redeeming A Prodigal

"Healing A Soul"

WHEN a man is born again he is capable of doing things entirely contrary to his natural life and impulse, even though the consequences are known to be as the most bitter of fruit, or as a punishment that lingers like a festering thorn in tender flesh. The born again experience attunes a man to the moral universe, convicts him of sin, quickens his spirit, and makes his conscience a thousand times more sensitive than it has ever been in its former state.

The man stood beside Pastor Brown's desk, ringing his hat, a shy, hesitant fellow, leaning upon first one leg and then the other. "I don't know why I'm here, Mr. Brown," he said.

He had been over at the filling station. The attendant there, a member of the Pastor's church, had told him about Pastor Brown, and urged him to seek counsel from the Pastor.

"If I can help you any," the Pastor promised, "you can count on me. What is the trouble? I can see you're in need."

In awkward, lumpy accents the man confessed that he was following a crooked line of business. When he had finished with his story Pastor Brown began to talk about the spiritual life.

"I'm not a Christian, Mr. Brown. I've never had much use for Christ, or for Christian people. Mother was a Christian, though." This last sentence brought a tenderness to his voice. "Mother's dead."

"Is she?" the Pastor asked, a curious note in his question.

"Yes," he repeated.

"It isn't quite logical to think of a Christian as dead," the Pastor added. "Some are dead even while they seem to be living. Was your mother a devoted Christian?"

"Oh, yes, Mr. Brown." He was on a subject close to his heart. And he spoke warmly and at length about the genuine quality of his mother's religion.

"Would your mother want you to be in this business?" asked Pastor Brown.

The man lowered his head. "No. She would be heart-broken if she knew."

"Then she is heart-broken," the Pastor said. "For she lives. She knows. And she prays for you. You must believe this. Your very soul depends on it."

It happened quickly. They were on their knees together seeking forgiveness and cleansing for this man's heart. And there on his knees he surrendered his life to Jesus, pouring out his soul in frank and honest repentance, supplication, and faith. When they rose the man's face was wet with tears of joy, for the glow on his face testified to the fact that he had been born again.

As the man made ready to leave he paused at the door and said: "Thank you, Mr. Brown. I may be at your prayer meeting tomorrow night, God willing."

"The next evening," said the Pastor, "all during our meeting, I kept watching the door. When the man failed to show up my heart sank. Could I have been deceived into believing the man redeemed? Why hadn't he come?"

On the following day Pastor Brown went to the address

he had given in search of him. But he had left the day before, leaving no forwarding address. He had disappeared from sight as completely as if he had dropped into the ocean. For many months the man remained in the Pastor's thought and prayer and Love. Then gradually he dropped from memory and was entirely forgotten.

It was five years later that the man stood once more beside the Pastor's desk.

"I guess you don't remember me, Mr. Brown," he said. "I was born again here five years ago. I have come back to see the place where I found my Savior."

The Pastor could not quite place him. His face was radiant and full of smiles. He chatted with ease and self-assurance, and every moment or so a pointed piece of scripture would come in to punctuate his conversation. Eventually he mentioned the circumstances that brought him to the Pastor's remembrance. With this there was a feast of fellowship, and the man filled in the vacant years.

The day following his conversion the man had set out for St. Louis, Missouri, where he gave himself up to the police. He had spent these five years in prison, a punishment voluntarily and gladly accepted.

In prison he had joined the Fishermen's Club and began to study the Bible, memorizing passage after passage in his cell. He talked with many men about Christ, and had the joy of leading others to the Great Emancipator. After leaving prison he had joined the Salvation Army, and gave his testimony in their street meetings.

"And now I'm back here to thank you again, Mr. Brown," he said, "for putting me straight that day when you prayed me through to my Blessed Lord and Savior."

Yes, men will do strange, right things after they have met the Master on their own private Damascus Road.

Chapter XXXII . . . .

Believe It Or Not

"Extracting Bullets By Prayer"

LAWRENCE was wounded at Okinawa shortly after the war ended. During the mopping-up period of the island battle a bullet, evidently intended for another target, entered the tent where Lawrence was sleeping and tore its way through several organs of his body.

Four operations were performed. Then the wounded man was brought home. He was in the Gardner General Hospital When Pastor Brown saw him. The Pastor described the meeting in these words:

"The sight of Lawrence shocked me and filled me with compassion. He was emaciated beyond human form, a living skeleton. I prayed with him and went away, sick at heart. But on my next visit I was overjoyed at his great improvement. The flesh was beginning to fill out in his face and he was feeling fine, as he put it.

"During the following weeks I prayed with him many times. His progress was steady. In a little while he was to be discharged from the hospital. After a good rest at home he was then to have his fifth operation, a sort of general repair job, so that he would not have to wear a colostomy. Then following his recovery from this he was to have his sixth and last operation.

"But this sixth operation was in the nature of a doubtful climax. Now the surgeons would attempt to extract the bullet from his body. In every previous operation they had been unable to do this because of profuse bleeding, and because the bullet was so deeply imbedded. It was to be a crucial operation.

"On my last visit to the hospital the lad's mother was present. Lawrence was the picture of health, as the saying goes. It was just before he was to be discharged. I said, 'Let's express our thanks to God in prayer, and give wings to our gratitude for the marvelous way He has blessed Lawrence, so far, on his way to complete recovery.'

"We all believed that this rapid progress had been due to something more than medical treatment, wonderful as that had been. And so I prayed a prayer of gratitude. As far as I remember there was not a single line of intercession in my prayer. Every word was an expression of thankfulness and praise.

"That was at four o'clock in the afternoon. Early the next morning the soldier discovered that the dressing over the wound where the bullet entered his body was wet. He called the nurse to investigate. She redressed the wound. But just before leaving him she suddenly exclaimed, 'What's this?' And she leaned over and picked up the bullet.

"It was a 31 caliber Japanese bullet. It was bent, indicating that it had struck some object, glanced off, and had gone through the tent and into the sleeping soldier's body.

"The patient immediately became the most talked of man in the hospital. Doctors and nurses, out of curiosity, journeyed to his bedside to gaze in frank wonderment. They would look at the bullet and then at the patient. No one in the hospital had ever witnessed a miracle of this kind. Shortly after the prayer of gratitude, the bullet had actually rolled out of the man's body."

"Pastor Brown," I said, "in all these cases of answered

prayer you seem to use quite a variety of methods. Is there any particular pattern of prayer or form of ritual that you especially lean upon?"

"I am not limited or bound to any form of prayer or ritual," he replied, simply. "I suppose I do use some methods of prayer more than others, and I suppose at times some people might think that a bit of ritual enters into them—but form and ritual are subordinate in my thinking. The one thing that I try to have is an inner stillness, a sense of oneness with God and a realization that His healing forces are always available. I feel that if I but yield myself wholly and completely to Him I may become an instrument through which His grace may flow. I know that prayer to be effective must rise from infinite faith and be borne by compassionate love. When I am filled with such an inner stillness, with such faith in God, and with such Love, I try to be led by the Holy Spirit so that I become "prayed through" by the Spirit and released so I may follow any pattern of prayer He directs. Thus it is the Spirit behind and through the prayer and not the prayer form that is of primary importance.

"The same applies to ritual. Many times my praying takes a very simple form: getting still; becoming one with God; interceding; expressing gratitude to God; and an outward seeming to "do" nothing. Sometimes I respond to the inner urge to do a very natural act such as laying my hand on the patient's head, wrist or affected part."

At this point I interrupted him with another question, "Do you feel that the laying on of hands in any way tends to strengthen the faith of the patient?"

"Yes," he replied, "I feel that ofttimes the faith of the patient is increased. The laying on of hands is a concrete act and the patient participates in the experience physically. On the mental level, there is definite psychological value whenever a patient has a lever he can grasp and can later recapture through memory. Most patients know that Jesus healed the sick and afflicted as he laid his hands upon them and that he instructed his disciples to heal that way. They know that through the ages healing has often come that way. Thus they are expectant. But not only that: I often experience some physical or mystical manifestation when I lay my hand upon a patient as I pray for him. And many patients have told me that they have experienced a physical or mystical manifestation while my hands were on them. And that strengthens their faith.

"Frequently when I lay my hand upon a person and pray, a strong vibration comes in my hand; sometimes a definite warmth. At no time am I able to create these physical sensations that come and go. I cannot bring them on, nor can I cast them off. And I am fundamentally unconcerned whether they are present or not. I have found that prayer is just as redemptive without them. In addition to these physical sensations, or even in their absence, I frequently have a sense of great peace and quietness in my heart while praying and upon leaving the patient feel spiritually exalted. And the joy of the experience lingers.

"The patient frequently comments about the sensation of marked warmth that my touch gives; or the tingling sensation he experiences, like electricity; or the feeling that he is being lifted up; or that he feels relaxed and in a state of perfect peace; or that he "knows" something has happened and that all will be well.

"Whenever there are these physical or mystical manifestations I believe God has done something and my heart sings with joy and gratitude for the greatness of His Love."

Chapter XXXIII . . . .

Refined In The Mint Of God

"The Training Of Pastor Brown"

AND now we come to the final question: what is the secret of Pastor Brown? How did he achieve such power of healing? How did he develop such faith in the promises of God? What fanned into flame such burning compassion for his fellow men?

One might as well ask, How is gold refined? A visitor to the United States mint was watching one day the gold being prepared, for pouring into molds, and growing impatient, he turned to the Master of the mint and asked, "How can you tell when the gold is ready for pouring?"

"When the heat becomes so intense that I can see the reflection of my face in the molten gold," was the answer.

The secret of Pastor Brown's spiritual power is all summed up in that sentence. He went through a refining process that continued until the Master's face began to be reflected in his own face and heart and soul. Only after that could the events related in this book come to pass.

His ministry did not begin on a bed of roses. He did not step into a wealthy church with a large salary and a staff of efficient helpers all around him. After an apprenticeship of seven years as an assistant pastor to Dr. Melbourne P. Boynton, he stepped forth as a full pastor into a little church that was burdened down with a $7,600 mortgage and $2,000 in unpaid bills and a background that was anything but promising.

"I certainly would never recommend any friend of mine to accept the pastorate of the Parkside Baptist Church." Such was the advice a friend gave him who had been a member of the church for many years. It was a church that had had a long line of pastors, many of whom had not served more than a year or two. The longest pastorate was less than six years. One of the earliest pastors was Dr. Edward Judson, son of the immortal Adoniram Judson who opened the way in Burma for the spreading of the gospel to the Burmese.

"The church started as a mission in 1894," said Pastor Brown, "and was not organized as a church until ten years later in 1904. At the time I became its pastor in 1932, it was going through deep waters of tribulation. Evil seemed to have a dominant hand, worldliness had crept into the hearts of some of the members, unkind thoughts about one another were being spoken. The Sunday before I preached my first sermon there, a member arose in the morning service and said, 'Folks, this is a divided church and the quicker one side gets out, the better.' And there was no mistaking which side he believed should get out.

"There had been a great deal of disharmony, jealousy, resentment, bitterness, unkindness, uncharitableness and even underhandedness toward one another. I knew that none of this belonged in a church. When I discovered how serious it was I knew what my friend had meant when he said he didn't want to see a friend of his accept it's pastorate. I didn't realize what I was getting into until I was in and then it became a challenge to me. Here was my opportunity to help people, And so for a year I preached about the human relationships of Christians to one another and bore down strongly upon the importance of Love among these of the household of faith. And Love grew.

"A year later I saw two deacons stand in the aisle, their hands clasped in brotherly Love, each looking deep into the eyes of the other as one said, 'Isn't it wonderful what God has done? I can hardly imagine that a year ago many of us were at each other's throats.' And a prayer of thanksgiving arose in my heart. As I look back upon the situation now I think of the church as an orchestra, with good musicians, each trying to play his instrument to the best of his ability. But the musicians were disregarding what others were playing. I had tried to be the conductor but had failed in my attempt to get all to play the same piece at the same time. It was not until another year had passed before we discovered the secret of our mistake. Some of us had been trying to run the church and we should have been letting Christ run the church. He was our Lord, He was the real Head of our church and we had been assuming some of His prerogatives. We had been trying to do ourselves what only He could do.

"At last I came to the end of my rope. I felt like Doctor E. Stanley Jones must have felt when I read later in his 'Christ of the Indian Road' how he had come to his Beãs, the place where Alexander had come and had turned back again; he could go no further. For Doctor Jones realized he could go no further until he had gone deeper. As I read these lines, they clicked, for it was my experience too. 'I could go no further until I had gone deeper.' Taking my Bible in my hands, I sat down and thought with compassion about the members of our church. My heart went out to them in Love and sympathy.

With great agony of soul I prayed to God that he would make me adequate for my task. Then I turned to the Bible and began reading at random. As I read I prayed that God would show me what the trouble was and how I could meet it. I was reading in the first epistle of John and as

I would read on my mind kept turning back to one particular verse. And so I found myself meditating on 1 John 1:9. 'If we confess our sins He is faithful and just to forgive us our sins, and to cleanse us from all unrighteousness.' I was sure God was speaking to the present situation. How did this apply to me?

"Through the years it was my custom to regularly confess sin to the Father and ask forgiveness and cleansing through the blood of Christ. But now my eyes were registering upon one particular word, a word that stood out as though it were printed in great black letters, a word that I had never seen in that verse before. It was the word 'all'. Why yes, in that very hour I had lost my patience when my little boy had gotten in my way, and I knew that was unrighteous. I confessed it as sin to God and asked his forgiveness. I thought again and remembered I had spoken unkindly to my wife that very evening. I realized that that was not righteous and that it was motivated by selfishness. So I confessed that as sin and asked God's forgiveness. And one by one I began to discover things in my life that were foreign to God's nature and to confess them to Him, seeking His forgiveness and promising to try to eliminate these things from my life.

"A whole flood of situations began to swarm into my memory. There was my temper, pride, conceit, resentments, self-righteousness, worry, fear and many other qualities that every Christian knows so well but usually is inclined to accept as human qualities that must be tolerated and overlooked, if not coddled. But here God was telling me that if I confess my sins to Him, He would cleanse me from 'all' unrighteousness. That was what I wanted, the complete cleansing. I knew that my repentence was sincere. Before I had finished praying a great peace came into my heart. It seemed as though my whole soul became flooded with the presence of the Holy Spirit. God had answered my prayer and for the first time I began to feel adequate for my ministry. I knew that *I must abide in Christ and Christ in me must motivate every thought and word and deed.*

"I telephoned two of the deacons to whom I felt close, Mr. W. H. Gresham and Mr. W. A. Diman II, and asked them if they would meet me at the church. They came wondering what was the trouble now. I set them at ease for I told them there was no trouble but that I had made a discovery and I wanted to share it with them. I related my experience and asked them to pray with me. I have ever since been grateful that God provided me with two such spirit-filled men for this crisis in my life. They comforted my heart and expressed joy in the spiritual blessing that had broken upon my soul. Then we prayed together and gave the church completely to God and its leadership completely to Jesus. I did not realize then the great significance of the experience I was having, or that that verse of Scripture would prove to be a turning point in my life.

"It was shortly after this that a friend presented me with 'The Lord's Prayer' by Professor Glenn Clark of Macalester College, St. Paul, Minn. Nothing in the book particularly impressed me due to the superficial reading I gave it. But the following day I remembered one little incident in it. It was the parable of the fanner-bees. For the next several days I kept thinking of it. Prof. Clark suggested an army of spiritual 'fanner-bees', aged people and shut-ins, who would pray thirty minutes a day for the nation. We had numbers of people in the church who were shut-ins, some were ill and some were elderly. I decided to ask them to become spiritual 'fanner-bees' and to spend thirty minutes each day praying for the church; just like the fanner-bees in a beehive which stand near the entrance to the hive with their heads 'bowed' and their wings moving constantly. This circulates the atmosphere, air-conditioning the hive causing the foul air to leave and fresh air to enter. We needed a new spiritual atmosphere in the church. Every person whom I asked to become a fanner-bee was thrilled at the opportunity for service. Mrs. Milton F. Pratt, one of our deaconesses, all but wept about it. She said, 'Pastor, in all my church experience, I never before had a pastor who asked me to pray for him or for the church.'

"They told me what time of the day or night they would pray. Within two weeks we had thirty-five 'fanner-bees' and it developed that at least one of these was praying for the church and its members every hour every day from five in the morning until midnight. Things soon began to happen, quietly and inconspicuously. Some people who were unhappy and critical became interested in other churches and a number transfered their membership from our fellowship. Some who had been indifferent to the church for years began to come back. A new Spirit was beginning to be felt in our midst.

"The next spring, I again was looking over this same little pamphet by Professor Clark and was intrigued by the description in the back of the book concerning the Camp Farthest Out at Lake Koronis. Here was a group of people earnestly seeking to go deeper in their spiritual life through prayer. I talked with my wife about it and made arrangements to go. Before the camp was over I found that I had something that was to become the great imperative in my life. I had become immersed in Christ, and doctrines, theology and experiences began to fall into a beautiful, harmonious and perfect pattern. My convictions concerning Christ and the Scriptures and the reality of the grace of God took on new meaning and brought me great joy. Even before we returned to Chicago, we had a number of marvelous experiences enroute. From then on I began to have a succession of answered prayer, the like of which I had never experienced before. Needs became fulfilled at the moment they were needed. Then one night

I had a marvelous vision.

"It was late Saturday night. The next morning I was to preach upon the text 'The Kingdom of Heaven is Within You.' I sat alone in our front room to meditate upon what Jesus meant when he made that statement. As I meditated, it seemed to me as though I stepped into a beautiful city. There were streets and boulevards, parks and trees and lagoons. There were marvelous buildings, some tall and stately and elegant. The streets were perfectly clean and the shrubbery and trees were a magnificent hue. But there was something strange about it all. I did not see a human being anywhere. Here was a city with not a soul present. There was a little chuckle at my side and I found myself looking into the eyes of a lad who appeared to me to be the most beautiful lad I had ever seen and my whole being responded to him with Love. Then he introduced himself to me and told me where I was. He said he had permitted me to enter his heart for he wanted to show me the things of his soul. I thought that was wonderful of the lad and I thrilled at the confidence and Love he had manifested in me. He took me throughout this Kingdom of his soul and into many buildings which represented his virtues and vices.

"At last we came to a magnificent palace whose brass doors swung automatically open and then closed behind us. I found that we were walking down a marble corridor with huge marble columns that led to a tremendously large room. At the further end, there was a dais on which was a throne chair. Together we walked across the room toward the dais but presently I found myself walking alone. A moment later I discovered that the lad was sitting in the chair. I continued to approach and then stood at the foot of the steps and looked up into his face. He smiled down upon me. He knew that I was bewildered by these things. In the midst of my wonderment I was conscious of a perfect harmony of Love and oneness between the two of us.

"Finally he spoke, 'You are in the Kingdom of my soul and this is my throne-room. Here I am king, absolute monarch and sovereign. Nothing can enter this kingdom except I give it permission—whether it be good or evil—for here I have absolute authority. I can admit or reject.'

"As he talked, there came a knock at the door. He turned his head and said, 'Who is there?' I could not hear the reply but the lad said, 'No you cannot enter.'

"Three times this happened and at last came another knock not as loud as the others. I had hardly heard it, but the lad said again, 'Who is there?'

"And I heard the reply, 'Jesus.'

"The lad glanced at me, then turned again in the direc- of the door; he hesitated, wondering what he should do. At last he said, 'Come in.'

"The door opened and Jesus stepped inside. The door closed behind Him. He remained standing just inside the door. He was dressed in the conventional garments of his day. It was noticeable that he did not advance until the lad invited Him to approach. He walked toward the place where I was standing. As He drew near, my heart leaped with joy as I saw that he recognized me. There was Love and understanding in His eyes. He didn't speak to me but He looked into my eyes with an expression that made me know that He knew me. He turned and looked up into the lad's face. For a long time the lad sat there as his eyes slowly filled with tears. Then he arose, descended the steps and sank to his knees in front of Jesus. Jesus radiated glory as He placed his hand upon the lad's head and blessed him. Then the lad arose and for several moments the two stood looking into each other's eyes and you could almost see the Love that flowed back and forth. Finally the lad turned, took Jesus by the arm and led Him up the stairs, turned Him around and motioned to Him to be seated. Jesus sat down upon the throne as the lad descended the steps, and kneeled before Him. After a while he arose and said, 'Here-to-fore I have been king of the kingdom of my soul, but I hereby abdicate my throne; I surrender it to You. From now on, whatever choices are to be made in my life are to be made according to Your will and not mine. Henceforth You are the King of the Kingdom of my Soul.'

"Just then a knock came at the door. The lad turned and said, 'Who's there?' He hesitated a moment and then said, 'It is up to Jesus; whatever He wishes shall be.' But Jesus shook His head without saying anything. It came to me like a flash. When Jesus enters us and takes the complete mastery, none of the little self-centered masters can enter again.

"One night following this vision, I had another vision of a terrible nature. For months I had been wrestling with a gigantic problem but found no solution. I determined to pray until an answer came. That night, I wrestled with my soul as Jacob of old and I was determined not to let go until God had done something.

"I do not know how long I had been upon my knees. It probably was several hours and I was still agonizing in prayer, when suddenly the head of a great serpent appeared before me and very slowly began moving nearer and nearer. Its eyes were like flames of fire and there was a fierceness in its appearance that was sufficient to frighten one to death. I had never seen or imagined such a fierce and ferocious thing in my life. I knelt there immovable with my gaze fixed upon its eyes. My whole soul surged in contempt. Very slowly the head drew closer to my face. The head itself was as large as my own. Its jaws were wide open and its fangs were bared and vibrating with anger. Soon I could feel the hot breath of its nostrils upon my face. It seemed as though its fangs would strike my cheek. Then I became aware of the fact that I was unafraid. There was absolutely no tension in my body.

I was perfectly calm as I knelt there looking into the face of this dreadful monster. And there was no tremor in my voice when I softly but positively said. 'You can't touch me.'

" 'No,' I said again, softly but authoritatively, 'You cannot touch me.' Though its fierceness was terrific I met its anger with a smile of confidence knowing that it was helpless and could come no farther and do no harm. Then it vanished.

"When I arose from prayer it was with fullness of heart and with joy unspeakable. I knew I had been victorious through Christ and that the problem I had wrestled with had vanished.

"From that time until this I have known that Satan is helpless in the presence of the Saviour and that when Christ speaks evil must obey."

CPSIA information can be obtained at www.ICGtesting.com
Printed in the USA
LVOW11s1928250814

400819LV00009B/1275/P